D0461063

Holiday COOKING VOLUME 6

DIABETIC LIVING® HOLIDAY COOKING IS
PART OF A BOOK SERIES PUBLISHED BY
BETTER HOMES AND GARDENS SPECIAL
INTEREST MEDIA, DES MOINES, IOWA

The holidays always bring my family closer.

When the air turns cold and the snow starts to fly in the Midwest, we slow down to spend time in our favorite place—home. My daughter and I often head to the kitchen. We dig through my late mom's recipe box for our old favorites and look at holiday editions of magazines and cookbooks for new ones.

I'm constantly on the lookout for recipes that cut back on calories and fat. This new volume of healthful, holiday-special recipes is a great place to find them. Just like each issue of *Diabetic Living*® magazine, this book is jam-packed with a collection of lightened-up dishes that will fit your meal plan and please everyone around the table.

My family loves desserts, so I look for recipes that satisfy them without derailing my efforts for all of us to eat more healthfully. These are some of my new favorites.

- Our Best Traditional Pumpkin Pie, *page 140*, has just 187 calories per serving and only 30 grams carb instead of 449 calories and 49 grams carb! Creamy and spiced just right, this pie serves up everything you want in a holiday dessert.
- Cranberry Champagne Coconut Snowball Cakes, *page 137*, led some food professionals around the Test Kitchen table to exclaim it's "the best dessert ever!"
- Maple-Bourbon Chocolate Tiramisu with Pecans, *page 150*, is a fresh take on a classic that had tasters going back again and again for "just one more bite."

This new collection offers dishes for every course. And you will find delicious—and easy-prep—slow cooker appetizers and one-bowl meals sprinkled throughout "Tasty Party Bites," *pages 26–47*, and "Comforting Soups and Stews," *pages 48–63*.

Diabetes doesn't have to disrupt your holiday traditions. Find some new recipes in *Holiday Cooking*, then prepare them for those you love.

Enjoy the season!

Martha

Martha Miller Johnson
Editor, *Diabetic Living*® magazine

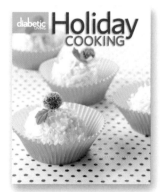

ON THE COVER:

Cranberry Champagne Coconut Snowballs
recipe on page 137

Photographer: Jason Donnelly

Diabetic Living
editorial advisory board

The following health care experts review articles that appear in *Diabetic Living*® magazine:

Nicholas Argento, M.D., PWD type 1, is the diabetes technology and electronic medical records director and a senior partner at Maryland Endocrine PA. He is the diabetes program medical advisor for Howard County General Hospital.

Connie Crawley, M.S., RD, LD, is a nutrition and health specialist for the University of Georgia Cooperative Extension in Athens, specializing in diabetes and weight loss.

Marjorie Cypress, Ph.D., CNP, CDE, is a diabetes nurse practioner in the department of endocrinology at ABQ Health Partners in Albuquerque. She is the vice president of Health Care and Education for the American Diabetes Association.

Marion J. Franz, M.S., RD, LD, CDE, has authored more than 200 publications on diabetes, nutrition, and exercise, including core-curriculum materials for diabetes educators.

Joanne Gallivan, M.S., RD, is executive director of the National Diabetes Education Program at the National Institutes of Health.

Frank Greenway, M.D., is head of outpatient research and professor at Pennington Biomedical Research Center of the Louisiana State University System.

Sharonne Hayes, M.D., FACC, FAHA, is a cardiologist and founder of the Women's Heart Clinic at Mayo Clinic in Rochester, Minnesota. She maintains an active medical practice focusing on preventive cardiology and heart disease in women.

Marty Irons, R.Ph., CDE, practices at a community pharmacy and also served in industry and the military. He also presents at diabetes education classes and is an author.

Irene B. Lewis-McCormick, M.S., CSCS, is a fitness presenter and is certified by leading fitness organizations. She is an author, educator, and faculty member of the American Council on Exercise, SCWFitness, SFR, and Upper Iowa University.

Chef Art Smith, star of Bravo's *Top Chef Masters* and former personal chef for Oprah Winfrey, has type 2 diabetes. He's the winner of two James Beard awards and founder of Common Threads, which teaches healthful cooking to low-income kids.

Hope S. Warshaw, M.S., RD, CDE, BC-ADM, is a writer specializing in diabetes care. She has authored several American Diabetes Association books.

John Zrebiec, M.S.W., CDE, is director of Behavioral Health Services at the Joslin Diabetes Center in Boston and a lecturer in the department of psychiatry at Harvard Medical School.

CONSUMER MARKETING

Vice President, Consumer Marketing	JANET DONNELLY
Consumer Marketing Product Director	HEATHER SORENSEN
Consumer Marketing Product Manager	WENDY MERICAL
Business Director	RON CLINGMAN
Production Manager	AL RODRUCK
Contributing Project Manager	SHELLI McCONNELL, PURPLE PEAR PUBLISHING, INC.
Contributing Photographer	JASON DONNELLY
Contributing Food Stylist	JENNIFER PETERSON
Test Kitchen Director	LYNN BLANCHARD
Test Kitchen Product Supervisors	JANE BURNETT, RD, LD; CARLA CHRISTIAN, RD, LD
Editorial Assistants	LORI EGGERS, MARLENE TODD

SPECIAL INTEREST MEDIA

Editorial Director	JIM BLUME
Art Director	GENE RAUCH
Managing Editor	DOUG KOUMA

DIABETIC LIVING® MAGAZINE

Editor	MARTHA MILLER JOHNSON
Art Director, Health	MICHELLE BILYEU
Senior Editor, Food & Nutrition	JESSIE SHAFER
Assistant Editor	LORI BROOKHART-SCHERVISH

MEREDITH NATIONAL MEDIA GROUP

President TOM HARTY

Chairman and Chief Executive Officer STEPHEN M. LACY

Vice Chairman MELL MEREDITH FRAZIER

In Memoriam — E.T. MEREDITH III (1933-2003)

Diabetic Living® Holiday Cooking is part of a series published by Meredith Corp., 1716 Locust St., Des Moines, IA 50309-3023.

If you have comments or questions about the editorial material in *Diabetic Living*® *Holiday Cooking*, write to the editor of *Diabetic Living* magazine, Meredith Corp., 1716 Locust St., Des Moines, IA 50309-3023. Send an e-mail to diabeticlivingmeredith.com or call 800/678-2651. magazine is available by subscription or on the newsstand. To order a subscription to magazine, go to *DiabeticLivingOnline.com*

© Meredith Corporation 2013. All rights reserved.

First edition. Printed in U.S.A.

ISSN 1943-2887   ISBN 978-0-696-30157-5

contents

Fennel-Orange Chicken with
Roasted Beets and Grapes
recipe on page 80

eye-opening
breakfasts

The aroma of one of these scrumptious dishes—waffles, quiche,

egg casserole, coffee cake, and more—wafting throughout the

house adds holiday cheer to a special breakfast or brunch. Each

one serves up a fresh, healthful, eye-appealing start to the day.

Apple-Cheddar Ham and Egg Casserole

Look for a medium-size fennel bulb. Once trimmed, cored, and chopped, it should yield 1 cup. The feathery fronds make a holiday-green garnish.

SERVINGS 8 ($^1/_8$ portion each)
CARB. PER SERVING 20 g
PREP 30 MINUTES
BAKE 50 minutes
STAND 10 minutes

- 6 ounces dry rye bread, cut into small cubes*
- 1 medium fennel bulb
- 6 ounces thinly sliced cooked lower-sodium ham, chopped
- 1 cup chopped cooking apple
- 1 cup shredded reduced-fat cheddar cheese (4 ounces)
- $^1/_2$ cup thinly sliced green onions (4)
- $1^1/_2$ cups refrigerated or frozen egg product, thawed, or 6 eggs, lightly beaten
- 2 cups fat-free milk
- $^1/_4$ teaspoon black pepper
- Sliced green onions (optional)

1 | Preheat oven to 325°F. Grease a 2-quart rectangular baking dish. Spread half of the bread cubes in the dish. If desired, snip some of the green feathery tops from the fennel bulb and reserve for a garnish. Trim, core, and chop fennel bulb to make 1 cup. Sprinkle fennel evenly over bread in dish. Top with ham, apple, cheese, and $^1/_2$ cup green onions. Top with remaining bread.

2 | In a medium bowl whisk together eggs, milk, and pepper. Drizzle evenly over bread mixture in dish. Press down lightly with the back of a large spoon so all the bread is moistened

3 | Bake, uncovered, for 50 to 60 minutes. Edges will be set and the center will appear runny. Let stand 10 minutes before serving to let center become set. If desired, sprinkle top with reserved fennel fronds and/or additional sliced green onions.

*TEST KITCHEN TIP: To dry bread, let bread cubes stand at room temperature for 6 hours. Or bake bread cubes in a 300°F oven for 8 to 10 minutes or until dry.

4 grams fat

PER SERVING: 180 cal., 4 g total fat (2 g sat. fat), 20 mg chol., 522 mg sodium, 20 g carb. (2 g fiber, 8 g sugars), 16 g pro. Exchanges: 1 vegetable, 1 starch, 2 lean meat, 0.5 fat.

Bacon-Pea-Swiss Scramble

Reduce the fat in this fold-together egg dish by substituting $\frac{1}{4}$ cup refrigerated or frozen egg product for each egg.

SERVINGS 2 ($\frac{3}{4}$ cup each)
CARB. PER SERVING 5 g
START TO FINISH 25 minutes

Nonstick cooking spray

2 slices turkey bacon, cut crosswise into thin strips

3 eggs

2 tablespoons reduced-sodium chicken broth

$\frac{1}{4}$ to $\frac{1}{2}$ teaspoon Asian chili sauce

$\frac{1}{4}$ cup frozen green peas, thawed and drained

$\frac{1}{4}$ cup grape or cherry tomatoes, quartered

2 tablespoons finely shredded Swiss cheese

2 teaspoons snipped fresh parsley

1 Coat an unheated medium nonstick skillet with cooking spray. Preheat skillet over medium heat. Add bacon and cook about 2 minutes or until browned. Remove bacon and set aside; discard any drippings from skillet. Return skillet to medium-low heat.

2 In a medium bowl whisk together the eggs, broth, and chili sauce. Stir in bacon and peas.

3 Pour egg mixture into hot skillet. Cook over medium-low heat, without stirring, until mixture begins to set on the bottom and around edges. With a spatula, lift and fold the partially cooked egg mixture so the uncooked portion flows underneath. Continue cooking until almost set. Fold in tomatoes, cheese, and parsley. Cook about 30 seconds more or until egg mixture is cooked through but is still glossy and moist. Serve immediately.

15 grams protein

PER SERVING: 194 cal., 12 g total fat (5 g sat. fat), 302 mg chol., 372 mg sodium, 5 g carb. (1 g fiber, 2 g sugars), 15 g pro. Exchanges: 2 medium-fat meat, 0.5 fat.

QUICK TIP
Crack each egg into a small custard cup or dish. The cup helps guide the egg into the just-right spot when pouring it into the hash.

Spicy Sausage and Sweet Potato Hash

Jump-start prep by peeling, cubing, and cooking the sweet potato the day before. Transfer it to an airtight container and refrigerate until ready to use.

SERVINGS 2 (1 cup hash and 1 egg each)
CARB. PER SERVING 18 g
START TO FINISH 25 minutes

1   small sweet potato, peeled and cut into $1/2$-inch cubes (about 1 cup)

$1/2$ cup water

$1/8$ teaspoon kosher salt

4   ounces uncooked turkey sausage links, chopped or crumbled

$1/4$ cup chopped red onion

2   to 3 tablespoons water

1   teaspoon Worcestershire sauce

1   teaspoon balsamic vinegar

$1/2$ to 1 teaspoon Asian chili sauce

2   eggs

1   tablespoon snipped fresh Italian (flat-leaf) parsley

    Black pepper (optional)

PER SERVING: 232 cal., 10 g total fat (3 g sat. fat), 223 mg chol., 824 mg sodium, 18 g carb. (2 g fiber, 6 g sugars), 16 g pro. Exchanges: 1 starch, 2 medium-fat meat.

1 In a medium skillet combine sweet potato, $1/2$ cup water, and salt. Bring to boiling over medium-high heat; reduce heat. Simmer, covered, for 5 to 8 minutes or until sweet potato is just tender. Drain; set aside.

2 In the same skillet cook and stir sausage over medium heat about 4 minutes or until browned. Stir in onion and 2 to 3 tablespoons water, scraping up the browned bits from bottom of skillet. Cook, covered, for 2 to 4 minutes. Stir in sweet potato, Worcestershire sauce, vinegar, and chili sauce. Cook and stir until the potato is heated through; remove from heat.

3 Make two small wells in the hash mixture with the back of a wooden spoon. Crack one egg into a small dish; pour gently into one of the wells. Repeat with remaining egg.

4 Cover skillet and return to medium heat. Cook hash and eggs for 2 to 3 minutes or until the whites of the eggs are completely set and yolks begin to thicken. Remove skillet from heat. Sprinkle with parsley and, if desired, black pepper. To serve, remove hash and eggs with a spatula.

QUICK TIP
Another time, make
this quiche using
8 ounces shredded
cooked turkey. Skip
the cooking in Step 2;
just combine the
shredded cooked
turkey, green onions,
and spices.

Monterey-Turkey Quiche

Pass a dish of fresh refrigerated salsa so your guests can spoon it over the quiche as they wish.

SERVINGS 8 (1 wedge each)
CARB. PER SERVING 10 g
PREP 30 minutes
BAKE 50 minutes
STAND 10 minutes

Butter-flavor nonstick cooking spray

6 sheets frozen phyllo dough (14×9-inch rectangles), thawed

8 ounces ground turkey breast

½ cup thinly sliced green onions (4)

2 cloves garlic, minced

½ teaspoon ground cumin

¼ teaspoon paprika

⅛ teaspoon crushed red pepper

2½ cups refrigerated or frozen egg product, thawed, or 10 eggs, lightly beaten

½ cup light sour cream

⅓ cup fat-free milk

4 ounces reduced-fat Monterey Jack cheese, shredded (1 cup)

¼ cup snipped fresh cilantro

4 to 5 thin red sweet pepper rings

5 to 6 thin fresh poblano pepper rings*

PER SERVING: 172 cal., 6 g total fat (3 g sat. fat), 33 mg chol., 312 mg sodium, 10 g carb. (1 g fiber, 3 g sugars), 19 g pro. Exchanges: 0.5 starch, 3 lean meat.

1 Preheat oven to 325°F. Coat a 9-inch pie plate with cooking spray. Unfold phyllo dough; remove 1 sheet of the phyllo dough. (As you work, cover the remaining phyllo dough with plastic wrap to prevent it from drying out.) Coat the phyllo sheet with cooking spray. Top with a second sheet of the phyllo dough. Coat with cooking spray. Gently press into the pie plate, allowing ends to extend over edge of plate. Coat and layer another 2 sheets of the phyllo dough; place diagonally across phyllo in pie plate in a crisscross fashion. Repeat with remaining 2 sheets of the phyllo dough and cooking spray, placing phyllo dough rectangles in pie plate at an angle to completely cover bottom of pie plate. Turn under edges of phyllo dough to form an edge.

2 Coat an unheated large nonstick skillet with cooking spray; heat over medium heat. Add turkey, green onions, garlic, cumin, paprika, and crushed red pepper. Cook until turkey is no longer pink, stirring to break up turkey as it cooks.

3 In a medium bowl whisk together egg, sour cream, and milk until well combined. Stir in cheese. Spoon turkey mixture into phyllo-lined pie plate, spreading to an even layer. Sprinkle with half of the cilantro. Slowly pour egg mixture over turkey mixture in pie plate. Lay red sweet pepper and poblano pepper rings on top.

4 Bake, uncovered, for 50 to 55 minutes or until a knife inserted near center comes out clean. If necessary, cover edge of phyllo crust with foil for the last 10 minutes of baking to prevent overbrowning. Let quiche stand on a wire rack for 10 minutes before serving. Sprinkle with remaining 2 tablespoons cilantro and cut into eight wedges.

*TEST KITCHEN TIP: Because chile peppers contain volatile oils that can burn your skin and eyes, avoid direct contact with them as much as possible. When working with chile peppers, wear plastic or rubber gloves. If your bare hands do touch the peppers, wash your hands and nails well with soap and warm water.

Smoked Salmon Tartine with Avocado-Grapefruit Salsa

A tartine is an open-face French sandwich that usually includes a fancy spreadable topping like this creamy salmon mixture.

SERVINGS 4 (2 open-face sandwiches each)
CARB. PER SERVING 26 g
START TO FINISH 15 minutes

1	medium red grapefruit, peeled, sectioned, and seeded
½	of a medium avocado, seeded, peeled, and chopped
½	cup chopped, seeded cucumber
½	cup chopped watercress or arugula
4	ounces whole grain baguette-style French bread
½	cup light tub-style cream cheese, softened
2	tablespoons fat-free milk
½	teaspoon finely shredded lemon peel
⅛	teaspoon crushed red pepper
4	ounces hot-smoked salmon (not lox-style), skinned and flaked

1 For salsa, in a small bowl combine grapefruit sections, avocado, cucumber, and watercress; toss gently to combine.

2 Cut baguette diagonally into eight slices, making the slices as long as possible. Toast bread slices and set aside.

3 In a medium bowl stir together cream cheese, milk, lemon peel, and crushed red pepper until well combined. Gently stir in salmon. Spread salmon mixture evenly onto toasted bread slices. Spoon salsa evenly on top and serve immediately.

PER SERVING: 227 cal., 9 g total fat (4 g sat. fat), 22 mg chol., 549 mg sodium, 26 g carb. (4 g fiber, 8 g sugars), 12 g pro. Exchanges: 1 vegetable, 0.5 fruit, 1 starch, 1.5 lean meat, 1 fat.

Shrimp and Tomato Oatmeal Risotto

Steel-cut oats cook into a risottolike base for this stir-fried shrimp and Broccolini brunch-style entrée.

SERVINGS 8 (^{2}/3 cup oat mixture and ^{1}/2 cup shrimp mixture each)
CARB. PER SERVING 22 g
PREP 25 minutes
COOK 30 minutes

1 pound fresh or frozen peeled and deveined shrimp

4 cups water

^{1}/2 teaspoon salt

1^1/3 cups steel-cut oats

1^1/2 to 2 cups no-salt-added chicken broth

6 tablespoons finely shredded Parmesan cheese

2 teaspoons olive oil

2 cups Broccolini, cut into 1^1/2- to 2-inch pieces, or 2 cups broccoli florets

2 cups diced roma tomatoes

^{1}/4 teaspoon freshly ground black pepper

^{1}/8 teaspoon coarse salt

Snipped fresh basil

2 tablespoons finely shredded Parmesan cheese (optional)

PER SERVING: 189 cal., 5 g total fat (1 g sat. fat), 75 mg chol., 586 mg sodium, 22 g carb. (4 g fiber, 2 g sugars), 15 g pro. Exchanges: 1.5 starch, 2 lean meat.

1 Thaw shrimp, if frozen. Halve shrimp lengthwise; set aside. In a large saucepan bring the water to boiling. Add the ^{1}/2 teaspoon salt. Gradually add oats, stirring constantly. Return to boiling; reduce heat. Simmer, covered, for 25 to 30 minutes or until oats are done, stirring occasionally.

2 Add 1^1/2 cups of the chicken broth to the oat mixture. Bring to boiling; reduce heat. Simmer, uncovered, about 4 minutes or until mixture is a creamy consistency (be careful not to overcook). Add the 6 tablespoons Parmesan cheese to oat mixture, stirring until cheese is completely melted. If necessary, stir in enough of the remaining ^{1}/2 cup broth to make desired consistency.

3 Meanwhile, in a large nonstick skillet heat oil over medium heat. Add shrimp and Broccolini. Cook and stir about 3 minutes or until shrimp are opaque. Stir in tomatoes, pepper, and the ^{1}/8 teaspoon coarse salt.

4 Divide oat mixture among eight serving dishes. Spoon shrimp mixture over. Sprinkle with basil. If desired, garnish with the 2 tablespoons Parmesan cheese.

Roasted Vegetable Frittata

Cremini mushrooms are often referred to as baby portobellos. They are similar to traditional white button mushrooms but darker in color and richer in flavor.

SERVINGS 8 (1/8 frittata each)
CARB. PER SERVING 4 g
PREP 15 minutes
ROAST 15 minutes
BAKE 22 minutes
STAND 10 minutes

Nonstick cooking spray

1 cup thin red onion wedges

1 cup sliced fresh cremini mushrooms

1 cup red sweet pepper strips (1 medium)

2 teaspoons olive oil

¼ teaspoon coarse salt

¼ teaspoon black pepper

½ cup coarsely chopped fresh baby spinach

2 ounces goat cheese (chèvre)

24 egg whites, beaten, or 3 cups pasteurized liquid egg whites

2 tablespoons snipped fresh oregano

1 Preheat oven to 400°F. Lightly coat a 15x10x1-inch baking pan and a 3-quart rectangular baking dish with cooking spray. In a large bowl toss together onion, mushrooms, sweet pepper, olive oil, salt, and black pepper. Spoon evenly into prepared 15x10x1-inch baking pan. Roast for 15 to 20 minutes or until vegetables are tender. Reduce oven temperature to 325°F.

2 In a large bowl toss together roasted vegetable mixture and spinach. Spread in the prepared 3-quart baking dish. Dot with small pieces of the goat cheese. Pour the egg whites over the top.

3 Bake for 22 to 30 minutes or until a knife inserted in the center comes out clean. Let stand for 10 minutes before serving. Sprinkle with oregano.

4 grams fat

PER SERVING: 103 cal., 4 g total fat (2 g sat. fat), 6 mg chol., 253 mg sodium, 4 g carb. (1 g fiber, 3 g sugars), 13 g pro. Exchanges: 0.5 vegetable, 2 lean meat.

QUICK TIP
To toast coconut, spread it in a baking pan. Bake in a 350°F oven for 5 to 10 minutes or until lightly browned, stirring once or twice.

Fresh Fruit Yogurt Soufflés

Coconut sugar is becoming a popular form of sweetener. Look for it at natural food stores or Asian markets

SERVINGS 8 (1 individual soufflé each)
CARB. PER SERVING 18 g
PREP 20 minutes
BAKE 20 minutes

Nonstick cooking spray

- ½ cup coconut sugar
- ⅔ cup pureed fresh or frozen raspberries or strawberries*
- ⅔ cup plain fat-free Greek yogurt
- 8 egg whites (1¼ cups)
- ¼ cup toasted coconut

PER SERVING: 98 cal., 1 g total fat (1 g sat. fat), 0 mg chol., 69 mg sodium, 18 g carb. (2 g fiber, 15 g sugars), 6 g pro. Exchanges: 1 fruit, 1 lean meat.

1 Preheat oven to 400°F. Lightly coat eight 8-ounce individual soufflé dishes with cooking spray. Using ¼ cup of the coconut sugar, coat the interiors of the soufflé dishes. Set aside.

2 In a small bowl stir together the pureed fruit and yogurt until well mixed. Set aside.

3 In a large bowl beat egg whites with an electric mixer on medium speed until soft peaks form (tips curl). Gradually add the remaining ¼ cup coconut sugar, beating until stiff peaks form (tips stand straight). Gently fold egg whites into fruit-yogurt mixture. Divide evenly among the prepared soufflé dishes. Sprinkle with toasted coconut.

4 Place soufflé dishes in a large baking pan. Place baking pan on oven rack. Pour boiling water into baking pan around soufflé dishes to a depth of 1 inch. Bake about 20 minutes or until a knife inserted near the centers comes out clean. Serve immediately.

*****TEST KITCHEN TIP:** You will need 1½ cups fresh berries to yield ⅔ cup puree.

Pumpkin Coffee Break Cake

Rather than wasting it, place the remaining pumpkin in an airtight container or freezer bag, seal, label, and freeze for another use.

SERVINGS 16 (1 slice each)
CARB. PER SERVING 29 g
PREP 30 minutes
BAKE 45 minutes
COOL 2 hours 20 minutes

Nonstick cooking spray

1 cup all-purpose flour

1 cup white whole wheat flour

2½ teaspoons baking powder

2 teaspoons pumpkin pie spice*

1 teaspoon finely shredded orange peel

½ teaspoon salt

1 cup water

¾ cup canned pumpkin

1 cup sugar**

¼ cup canola oil

1 teaspoon vanilla-butter-nut flavoring or 2 teaspoons vanilla

4 egg whites or ½ cup refrigerated or frozen egg substitute, thawed

¾ cup chopped pecans, toasted

½ cup orange juice

2 tablespoons sugar**

1½ teaspoons cornstarch

¼ teaspoon vanilla-butter-nut flavoring or ½ teaspoon vanilla

Orange slices (optional)

1 | For cake, preheat oven to 325°F. Generously coat a 10-inch nonstick fluted tube pan with cooking spray; set aside. In a medium bowl combine all-purpose flour, white whole wheat flour, baking powder, pumpkin pie spice, orange peel, and salt; set aside. In a small bowl combine the water and pumpkin.

2 | In a large bowl combine the 1 cup sugar, the oil, and the 1 teaspoon flavoring. Beat with an electric mixer on medium-high speed until well mixed. Add egg whites, one at a time, beating well after each addition. Alternately add flour mixture and pumpkin mixture to beaten mixture, beating on low speed after each addition just until combined.

3 | Sprinkle pecans in the bottom of the prepared pan. Carefully pour batter evenly over pecans. Bake for 45 to 50 minutes or until a wooden pick inserted in center of cake comes out clean. Cool in the pan on a wire rack for 20 minutes. Invert pan and cake together. Remove pan. Cool cake on wire rack for at least 2 hours.

4 | Meanwhile, for glaze, in a small saucepan combine orange juice, the 2 tablespoons sugar, and the cornstarch; stir until cornstarch is completely dissolved. Cook and stir over medium-high heat until boiling; cook and stir for 1 minute more. Remove from heat. Stir in the ¼ teaspoon flavoring. Cool completely.

5 | Just before serving, drizzle cooled glaze evenly over top of cooled cake. If desired, garnish with orange slices.

*TEST KITCHEN TIP: If desired, substitute 1 teaspoon ground cinnamon, ½ teaspoon ground nutmeg, ¼ teaspoon ground allspice, and ¼ teaspoon ground ginger for the pumpkin pie spice.

**SUGAR SUBSTITUTES: We do not recommend using a sugar substitute for this recipe.

3 grams protein

PER SERVING: 189 cal., 7 g total fat (1 g sat. fat), 0 mg chol., 164 mg sodium, 29 g carb. (2 g fiber, 16 g sugars), 3 g pro. Exchanges: 1 starch, 1 carb., 1 fat.

Pear, Ginger, and Pecan Mini Muffins

Two of these bite-size treats make a serving. Serve them alongside a veggie-filled egg white omelet for a complete breakfast.

SERVINGS 18 (2 mini muffins each)
CARB. PER SERVING 19 g or 16 g
PREP 30 minutes
BAKE 10 minutes
COOL 5 minutes

Nonstick cooking spray

1½ cups flour

½ teaspoon baking powder

¼ teaspoon baking soda

¼ teaspoon ground ginger

⅛ teaspoon salt

½ cup sugar*

⅓ cup pear juice or apple juice

¼ cup vegetable oil

1 egg, lightly beaten

1 large Bosc pear (about 8 ounces), peeled, cored, and chopped

½ cup chopped pecans, toasted

¼ cup finely chopped crystallized ginger

PER SERVING: 132 cal., 6 g total fat (1 g sat. fat), 10 mg chol., 53 mg sodium, 19 g carb. (1 g fiber, 7 g sugars), 2 g pro. Exchanges: 1 starch, 1 fat.

PER SERVING WITH SUBSTITUTE: Same as above, except 124 cal., 16 g carb. (5 g sugars).

1 Preheat oven to 400°F. Coat thirty-six 1¾-inch muffin cups with cooking spray; set aside.

2 In a medium bowl whisk together flour, baking powder, baking soda, ground ginger, and salt. In another bowl whisk together sugar, pear juice, oil, and egg until well mixed. Pour juice mixture into flour mixture; whisk just until smooth. Fold in chopped pear, pecans, and 2 tablespoons of the crystallized ginger. Spoon into the prepared muffin cups. Sprinkle with the remaining 2 tablespoons crystallized ginger.

3 Bake for 10 to 12 minutes or until a toothpick inserted in the centers of muffins comes out clean. Cool in muffin cups on a wire rack for 5 minutes. Remove from muffin cups. Serve while warm or cooled.

*SUGAR SUBSTITUTES: Choose from Splenda Sugar Blend for Baking or bulk C&H Light Sugar & Stevia Blend. Follow package directions to use product amount equivalent to ½ cup sugar.

Buckwheat-Blueberry Muffins

Rather than cooking your own squash, pick up a package of frozen butternut squash. Thaw enough squash to equal 1 cup; press out liquid.

SERVINGS 12 (1 muffin each)
CARB. PER SERVING 24 g or 22 g
PREP 20 minutes
BAKE 17 minutes
COOL 5 minutes

Nonstick cooking spray

¾ cup buckwheat flour

⅔ cup spelt flour or whole wheat flour

⅔ cup all-purpose flour

¼ cup sugar*

1½ teaspoons baking powder

1 teaspoon ground cinnamon

½ teaspoon baking soda

½ teaspoon salt

2 eggs, lightly beaten

1 cup mashed cooked butternut squash

½ cup fat-free milk

½ teaspoon finely shredded orange peel

¼ cup orange juice

2 tablespoons vegetable oil

¾ cup fresh or frozen blueberries

1 to 2 tablespoons regular rolled oats

1 | Preheat oven to 400°F. Coat twelve 2½-inch muffin cups with cooking spray or line with paper bake cups. If using paper bake cups, coat insides of paper cups with cooking spray; set pan aside.

2 | In a large bowl combine the buckwheat flour, spelt flour, all-purpose flour, sugar, baking powder, cinnamon, baking soda, and salt. Make a well in the center of flour mixture; set aside. In a medium bowl combine the eggs, squash, milk, orange peel, orange juice, and oil. Add the egg mixture all at once to the flour mixture. Stir just until moistened (batter should be lumpy). Fold in blueberries. Spoon batter into the prepared muffin cups, filling each almost full. Sprinkle with oats.

3 | Bake for 17 to 20 minutes or until a toothpick inserted in center of muffins comes out clean. Cool in muffin cups on a wire rack for 5 minutes. Remove from muffin cups. Serve while warm.

*SUGAR SUBSTITUTES: Choose from Splenda Sugar Blend or C&H Light Sugar & Stevia Blend. Follow package directions to use product amount equivalent to ¼ cup sugar.

PER SERVING: 145 cal., 4 g total fat (1 g sat. fat), 31 mg chol., 197 mg sodium, 24 g carb. (3 g fiber, 6 g sugars), 4 g pro. Exchanges: 1.5 starch, 0.5 fat.

PER SERVING WITH SUBSTITUTE: Same as above, except 139 cal., 22 g carb. (4 g sugars).

Pumpkin-Ricotta Pancakes

A bit of snipped fresh mint and fresh orange slices add a burst of flavor and a bright accent of color to this colors-of-fall stack.

SERVINGS 2 (3 pancakes and about 3 tablespoons topping each)
CARB. PER SERVING 43 g or 37 g
START TO FINISH 25 minutes

½ cup whole wheat pastry flour
1 teaspoon baking powder
½ teaspoon pumpkin pie spice
¼ teaspoon salt
2 egg whites
¼ cup unsweetened almond milk
¼ cup canned pumpkin
¼ cup part-skim ricotta cheese
1 tablespoon packed brown sugar*
1 tablespoon olive oil
1½ teaspoons finely shredded orange peel
½ teaspoon vanilla
½ teaspoon cider vinegar
1 medium orange
2 teaspoons honey
½ teaspoon snipped fresh mint
Nonstick cooking spray

1 In a medium bowl combine flour, baking powder, pumpkin pie spice, and salt. In another bowl use a fork to combine the egg whites, almond milk, pumpkin, ricotta, brown sugar, olive oil, 1 teaspoon of the orange peel, vanilla, and vinegar. Add pumpkin mixture to flour mixture. Stir just until moistened. Cover and let stand for 10 minutes.

2 Meanwhile, for orange topping, peel and section orange over a small bowl. Squeeze any juice from the membranes over the segments (about 2 tablespoons). Stir in honey, mint, and remaining ½ teaspoon orange peel. Set aside.

3 Spray an unheated griddle or heavy skillet with cooking spray. Pour about ¼ cup batter onto hot griddle or skillet. Using the back of a spoon, spread batter into 3- to 4-inch pancakes. Cook over medium heat for 1 to 2 minutes on each side or until pancakes are golden brown. Turn over when surfaces are bubbly and edges are slightly dry. Serve with orange topping.

*SUGAR SUBSTITUTES: Choose from Sweet'N Low Brown or Sugar Twin Granulated Brown. Follow package directions to use product amount equivalent to 1 tablespoon brown sugar.

PER SERVING: 303 cal., 10 g total fat (3 g sat. fat), 10 mg chol., 574 mg sodium, 43 g carb. (5 g fiber, 20 g sugars), 12 g pro. Exchanges: 0.5 fruit, 2 starch, 0.5 carb., 1 lean meat, 1 fat.

PER SERVING WITH SUBSTITUTE: Same as above, except 276 cal., 37 g carb. (14 g sugars). Exchanges: 0 carb.

Orange-Kissed Date Waffles

Waffle making success depends on the waffle maker. For crispy waffles, preheating the grids before adding the batter is necessary.

SERVINGS 12 (1 waffle [using ⅓ cup batter] each)
CARB. PER SERVING 27 g or 26 g
PREP 15 minutes
STAND 5 minutes

¾ cup boiling water

½ cup chopped, pitted Medjool dates

1¼ cups whole wheat pastry flour

½ cup all-purpose flour

1 tablespoon baking powder

1 tablespoon packed brown sugar*

2 teaspoons finely shredded orange peel

¼ teaspoon salt

½ cup refrigerated or frozen egg product, thawed, or 2 eggs

1 cup fat-free milk

¼ cup canola oil

1 teaspoon vanilla

4 navel, Cara Cara, and/or blood oranges

¾ cup reduced-calorie maple-flavored syrup, warmed (optional)

PER SERVING: 164 cal., 5 g total fat (0 g sat. fat), 0 mg chol., 200 mg sodium, 27 g carb. (3 g fiber, 11 g sugars), 4 g pro. Exchanges: 1 fruit, 1 starch, 1 fat.

PER SERVING WITH SUBSTITUTE: Same as above, except 160 cal., 26 g carb. (10 g sugars).

1 | In a small bowl combine boiling water and dates. Let stand for 5 minutes.

2 | Meanwhile, in a large bowl combine pastry flour, all-purpose flour, baking powder, brown sugar, orange peel, and salt. Make a well in the center of the flour mixture; set aside.

3 | Transfer undrained dates to a blender. Add eggs. Cover and blend until smooth. Add milk, oil, and vanilla. Cover and blend until combined. Add all at once to the flour mixture. Stir just until moistened (batter should be slightly lumpy).

4 | Add ⅓ cup batter to a preheated, lightly greased waffle baker according to manufacturer's directions (use a regular or Belgian waffle baker). Close lid quickly; do not open until done. Bake according to manufacturer's directions. When done, use a fork to lift waffle off grid. Place baked waffles in a warm oven (200°F to 250°F) while baking remaining waffles. Repeat making waffles with remaining batter.

5 | Cut ends off each orange. Set each orange on one end and use a sharp knife to cut off the peel and white pith. Thinly slice oranges crosswise into circles. Divide waffles among 12 serving plates. Top with orange slices. If desired, drizzle with syrup.

*SUGAR SUBSTITUTES: Choose from Sweet'N Low Brown or Sugar Twin Granulated Brown. Follow package directions to use product amount equivalent to 1 tablespoon brown sugar.

Mango Batidas

Look for agave nectar, an all-natural honeylike sweetener, near the sugar or in the health food section of the supermarket.

SERVINGS 8 ($^2/_3$ cup each)
CARB. PER SERVING 12 g
PREP 15 minutes
FREEZE 30 minutes

8 fresh raspberries

8 green grapes

8 pieces fresh mango

2 cups fresh mango pieces (about 9½ ounces)

2 cups light vanilla soymilk

2 teaspoons agave nectar

3 cups ice cubes

1 | Thread raspberries, grapes, and the 8 mango pieces onto eight short skewers. Place skewers in the freezer for 30 minutes or up to 24 hours.

2 | In a blender combine the 2 cups mango, the soymilk, and agave nectar. Add ice cubes. Cover and blend until smooth. Pour into eight stemmed glasses. Serve skewers with mixture in glasses.

PER SERVING: 57 cal., 1 g total fat (0 g sat. fat), 0 mg chol., 28 mg sodium, 12 g carb. (1 g fiber, 11 g sugars), 2 g pro. Exchanges: 1 fruit.

1 gram fat

QUICK TIP
Throughout the year, you will most likely find imported or domestic mango available. If ripe mangoes are not in the produce section, pick up a bag of frozen mango pieces to use in the smoothies.

tasty
party bites

From sizzling broiled skewers to crispy oven-baked veggie fries

and saucy slow-cooked sausage bites to chilly layered bean dip,

these scrumptious appetizers pack punch that's special enough

for the holidays. Lightened up and made healthful for you, each

is festive, flavorful, and fun to serve.

Prosciutto Asparagus Bites
with Avocado Spread

Use a long serrated knife and a sawing motion to cut the red and green filled tortilla wraps into 1-inch-thick slices.

SERVINGS 16 (2 pieces each)
CARB. PER SERVING 10 g
PREP 50 minutes
CHILL 30 minutes

1 medium avocado, halved and seeded

⅓ cup plain fat-free yogurt

¼ cup fresh basil leaves

2 tablespoons fresh cilantro leaves

1 tablespoon lemon juice

2 cloves garlic, minced

¼ teaspoon black pepper

12 ounces asparagus spears, woody bases removed

1 medium red sweet pepper, sliced

2 ounces very thinly sliced prosciutto

4 10-inch whole wheat flour tortillas

2 cups fresh arugula or spinach leaves

1 In a food processor combine avocado, yogurt, basil, cilantro, lemon juice, garlic, and black pepper. Process until smooth.

2 Bring a large pot of water to boiling. Add asparagus and sweet pepper. Return to boiling. Cook for 2 minutes. Drain vegetables and plunge into an ice water bath.

3 Cut prosciutto slices in half lengthwise. Spread avocado mixture onto tortillas, leaving a 1-inch space along one edge of each tortilla. Arrange prosciutto over avocado mixture. Top with arugula leaves. Place asparagus and red pepper slices on greens along the edge opposite the 1-inch space. Carefully roll up tortillas tightly, starting with the edge with the asparagus. Cover and chill for at least 30 minutes or for up to 4 hours.

4 To serve, cut each roll diagonally into eight approximately 1-inch-thick pieces.

PER SERVING: 82 cal., 3 g total fat (1 g sat. fat), 3 mg chol., 242 mg sodium, 10 g carb. (6 g fiber, 1 g sugars), 4 g pro. Exchanges: 0.5 vegetable, 0.5 starch, 0.5 fat.

4 grams protein

Cranberry-Citrus Meatballs

An orange and lime combo gives the classic cranberry-ketchup sauce a juicy, fresh flavor boost.

SERVINGS 32 (2 meatballs each)
CARB. PER SERVING 8 g
PREP 30 minutes
SLOW COOK 3 hours (low) or 1$^{1}/_{2}$ hours (high)

2 eggs, lightly beaten

2 pounds ground pork

1 cup cooked long grain brown rice

$^{1}/_{2}$ cup dried cranberries, finely chopped

1 teaspoon salt

$^{1}/_{4}$ teaspoon black pepper

2 to 3 teaspoons olive oil

1 14-ounce can whole-berry cranberry sauce

$^{1}/_{3}$ cup reduced-sugar ketchup

$^{1}/_{4}$ cup orange juice

2 tablespoons lime juice

PER SERVING: 103 cal., 5 g total fat (2 g sat. fat), 31 mg chol., 127 mg sodium, 8 g carb. (0 g fiber, 5 g sugars), 6 g pro. Exchanges: 0.5 fruit, 1 medium-fat meat.

1 In a large bowl combine eggs, pork, rice, dried cranberries, salt, and pepper. Shape mixture into 64 meatballs (each about 1$^{1}/_{2}$ inches in diameter). If mixture is sticky, use wet hands to shape the meatballs.

2 In an extra-large skillet heat 2 teaspoons of the oil over medium heat. Cook meatballs, half at a time, in hot oil about 5 minutes or just until browned and slightly firm (meatballs will not be cooked through), turning once halfway through cooking. If necessary, add the remaining 1 teaspoon oil to skillet during cooking. Immediately transfer meatballs to a 3$^{1}/_{2}$- or 4-quart slow cooker.

3 In a medium bowl whisk together cranberry sauce, ketchup, orange juice, and lime juice until combined. Pour cranberry sauce mixture over meatballs in slow cooker (do not stir). Cover; cook on low-heat setting for 3 to 4 hours or on high-heat setting for 1$^{1}/_{2}$ to 2 hours.

Tandoori-Spiced Chicken Pita Crisps with Cilantro Sauce

You can make the pita crisps the day ahead. Prepare them as directed, then place them in an airtight container, cover, and store at room temperature.

SERVINGS 24 (2 crisps each)
CARB. PER SERVING 7 g
PREP 35 minutes
MARINATE 4 hours
BAKE 20 minutes

½ cup plain fat-free Greek yogurt
¼ of a small onion
1 tablespoon lime juice
1 ½-inch piece fresh ginger, peeled
2 cloves garlic
1 teaspoon ground turmeric
¾ teaspoon salt
½ teaspoon ground coriander
½ teaspoon ground cumin
½ teaspoon black pepper
¼ teaspoon ground cinnamon
1½ pounds skinless, boneless chicken thighs
4 6-inch pita bread rounds
3 tablespoons canola oil
1 recipe Cilantro Sauce
Fresh cilantro leaves (optional)

1 For marinade, in a food processor combine yogurt, onion, lime juice, ginger, garlic, turmeric, ½ teaspoon of the salt, the coriander, cumin, pepper, and cinnamon. Cover and process until smooth. Transfer marinade to a medium bowl. Trim fat from chicken. Add chicken to marinade; toss to coat. Cover and marinate in the refrigerator for 4 hours, stirring once or twice.

2 Preheat oven to 350°F. Cut pita bread rounds in half horizontally; cut each half into six wedges, making 48 wedges total. In a large bowl combine pita wedges, 2 tablespoons of the oil, and the remaining ¼ teaspoon salt; toss to coat. Spread wedges on a baking sheet. Bake about 20 minutes or until crisp, turning twice.

3 Meanwhile, remove chicken from marinade, scraping off excess. Cut chicken crosswise into thin slices. In a large skillet heat the remaining 1 tablespoon oil over medium-high heat. Add chicken; cook and stir about 5 minutes or until no longer pink. Remove from heat. Using the edge of a metal spatula, break chicken into bite-size pieces.

4 To serve, place a small amount of chicken on each pita wedge. Top with a small spoonful of Cilantro Sauce. If desired, garnish with cilantro leaves.

CILANTRO SAUCE: In a food processor combine ½ cup lightly packed fresh cilantro leaves, ¼ cup cashews or pistachio nuts, 2 tablespoons lime juice, 2 tablespoons canola oil, 1 tablespoon rice wine vinegar, 2 cloves garlic, ½ teaspoon salt, ½ teaspoon finely chopped fresh serrano chile pepper (see tip, *page 33*) and ¼ teaspoon ground cumin. Cover and process until smooth.

PER SERVING: 100 cal., 5 g total fat (1 g sat. fat), 27 mg chol., 204 mg sodium, 7 g carb. (0 g fiber, 0 g sugars), 7 g pro. Exchanges: 0.5 starch, 1 lean meat, 0.5 fat.

Mini Souvlaki Skewers with Fennel-Yogurt Dip

Use the medium-tooth side of a box grater to shred the fresh fennel for the stir-together dip.

SERVINGS 12 (4 skewers and about 2 tablespoons dip each)
CARB. PER SERVING 5 g
PREP 30 minutes
BROIL 7 minutes

1½ pounds boneless pork loin chops, cut 1 inch thick

2 teaspoons finely shredded lemon peel

3 tablespoons lemon juice

2 tablespoons olive oil

3 cloves garlic, minced

1 teaspoon dried oregano, crushed

½ teaspoon black pepper

¼ teaspoon salt

4 cups grape tomatoes

1 medium seedless cucumber, halved lengthwise and sliced crosswise

Fresh oregano leaves (optional)

1 recipe Fennel-Yogurt Dip

PER SERVING: 120 cal., 4 g total fat (1 g sat. fat), 38 mg chol., 183 mg sodium, 5 g carb. (1 g fiber, 3 g sugars), 15 g pro. Exchanges: 1 vegetable, 2 lean meat.

1 Preheat broiler. Line a 15x10x1-inch baking pan with foil; set aside. Trim fat from meat. Cut meat into 1-inch pieces. Place meat in a large bowl.

2 In a small bowl combine lemon peel, lemon juice, oil, garlic, dried oregano, pepper, and salt. Pour half of the lemon mixture over meat; toss to coat. Spread meat in the prepared baking pan.

3 Broil 4 to 5 inches from the heat for 7 to 8 minutes or until meat is slightly pink in center (145°F), turning once. Drizzle with the remaining lemon mixture.

4 On cocktail picks, thread one piece of meat, one tomato, and a piece of cucumber. If desired, garnish with fresh oregano. Serve with Fennel-Yogurt Dip.

FENNEL-YOGURT DIP: In a small bowl combine 1 cup plain fat-free Greek yogurt; ½ cup grated fennel; 1 tablespoon lemon juice; ½ to 1 clove garlic, minced; ½ teaspoon salt; and dash cayenne pepper. Cover and chill until ready to serve.

Mango Habanero Pulled Chicken Bites

The sweet mangoes help tame the habanero heat, but use just one chile if you don't like food too spicy and hot.

SERVINGS 16 (3 tablespoons chicken mixture and 2 toasts each)
CARB. PER SERVING 19 g
PREP 25 minutes
SLOW COOK 4 hours (low) or 2 hours (high)

- 3 mangoes, peeled and seeded
- 1 to 2 fresh habanero chile pepper(s), seeded and chopped*
- ½ chopped onion
- ¼ cup low-calorie barbecue sauce
- 2 tablespoons honey
- 1 clove garlic, minced
- ¼ teaspoon black pepper
- 6 bone-in chicken thighs, skinned
- 1 8-ounce loaf baguette-style French bread, cut into 32 slices and toasted
- ¼ cup thinly sliced green onions (2)

PER SERVING: 113 cal., 1 g total fat (0 g sat. fat), 25 mg chol., 173 mg sodium, 19 g carb. (1 g fiber, 8 g sugars), 7 g pro. Exchanges: 0.5 fruit, 0.5 starch, 1 lean meat.

1 Chop two of the mangoes. In a food processor or blender combine chopped mangoes and chile pepper(s). Cover and process or blend until smooth.

2 In a 3½- or 4-quart slow cooker stir together the mango mixture, onion, barbecue sauce, honey, garlic, and black pepper. Add chicken thighs; stir to coat. Cover; cook on low-heat setting for 4 to 5 hours or on high-heat setting for 2 to 2½ hours.

3 Transfer chicken to a cutting board, reserving sauce in cooker. When cool enough to handle, remove chicken from bones; discard bones. Using two forks, pull meat apart into shreds; place meat in a large bowl. Add 1½ cups of the sauce from the cooker to the chicken in bowl; stir well to combine. Cut the remaining mango into 32 thin slices. Serve chicken mixture on top of toasted baguette slices. Garnish each with a mango slice and a sprinkle of green onions.

*TEST KITCHEN TIP: Because chile peppers contain volatile oils that can burn your skin and eyes, avoid direct contact with them as much as possible. When working with chile peppers, wear plastic or rubber gloves. If your bare hands do touch the peppers, wash your hands and nails well with soap and warm water.

QUICK TIP

Color doesn't determine the ripeness of a mango. Choose a mango by gently giving it a squeeze; if it gives slightly, it is ripe.

Boneless Buffalo Wings

Easy to eat, these baked chicken fingers that are crunchy on the outside and juicy on the inside boast the same great spicy flavor as the popular bar food.

SERVINGS 12 (2 chicken pieces, 1 carrot stick, 1 celery stick, and 4 teaspoons yogurt mixture each)
CARB. PER SERVING 11 g
PREP 30 minutes
BAKE 10 minutes

Nonstick cooking spray

3 tablespoons flour

¼ teaspoon black pepper

⅛ teaspoon salt

¼ cup low-fat buttermilk

2 tablespoons bottled lower-sodium Buffalo wing sauce, such as Wing Time brand

1 tablespoon honey

1 tablespoon Dijon-style mustard

1 cup whole wheat panko or panko (Japanese-style bread crumbs)

2 tablespoons whole-grain cornmeal

1 pound skinless, boneless chicken breast, cut into 4×1-inch pieces

¾ cup plain fat-free Greek yogurt

2 tablespoons bottled light blue cheese salad dressing

2 tablespoons crumbled blue cheese

12 carrot sticks

12 celery sticks

1 Preheat oven to 450°F. Lightly coat a 15×10×1-inch baking pan with cooking spray. In a shallow dish combine flour, pepper, and salt. In another shallow dish beat together buttermilk, buffalo wing sauce, honey, and mustard. In a third shallow dish combine panko and cornmeal. Dip each chicken piece into the flour mixture to coat. Transfer to the buttermilk mixture and toss to coat, draining off any excess mixture. Transfer to panko mixture and toss to coat. Place breaded chicken pieces on the prepared baking pan. Lightly coat breaded chicken pieces with cooking spray.

2 Bake for 10 to 15 minutes or until crisp and no longer pink, turning once halfway through baking.

3 Meanwhile, in a small bowl combine yogurt, salad dressing, and blue cheese. Serve chicken pieces with blue cheese-yogurt mixture. Serve with carrot and celery sticks.

*TEST KITCHEN TIP: Check the label for wing sauce that has 40 mg sodium or less per 2 tablespoons.

3 grams fat

PER SERVING: 114 cal., 3 g total fat (1 g sat. fat), 26 mg chol., 174 mg sodium, 11 g carb. (1 g fiber, 3 g sugars), 11 g pro. Exchanges: 0.5 starch, 1.5 lean meat.

Apricot-Honey Mustard Sausage Bites

If you wish to serve these glistening bites on a platter, use small decorative wooden picks and thread two sausage pieces and one apricot piece on each.

SERVINGS 32 (2 sausage slices and 1 apricot quarter each)
CARB. PER SERVING 7 g
PREP 15 minutes
SLOW COOK 3 hours (low) or 1½ hours (high)

- 2 12-ounce packages apple-flavor cooked chicken sausage links (8 links)
- ⅔ cup apricot preserves or sugar-free apricot preserves
- 8 dried apricots, quartered (about ½ cup)
- ⅓ cup chopped onion
- 3 tablespoons honey mustard
- 1 tablespoon water
- ½ teaspoon snipped fresh thyme

1 Bias-cut each sausage link into eight slices, making 64 slices total.

2 In a 2-quart slow cooker combine apricot preserves, dried apricots, onion, honey mustard, and the water. Add sausage, stirring to coat. Cover; cook on low-heat setting for 3 to 4 hours or on high-heat setting for 1½ to 2 hours. Just before serving, stir in thyme.

PER SERVING: 69 cal., 3 g total fat (1 g sat. fat), 15 mg chol., 217 mg sodium, 7 g carb. (0 g fiber, 5 g sugars), 3 g pro. Exchanges: 0.5 carb., 0.5 medium-fat meat.

Sole Cakes

The cakes are very soft, so handle them carefully and reshape them as necessary after coating them in the panko.

 SERVINGS 8 (1 sole cake and about 1 tablespoon yogurt mixture each)
CARB. PER SERVING 8 g
PREP 45 minutes
BAKE 12 minutes

Nonstick cooking spray

- 1 pound skinless sole or cod fillets
- 1 egg, lightly beaten
- 1 cup soft whole wheat bread crumbs
- 1 6-ounce carton plain fat-free Greek yogurt
- 2 tablespoons thinly sliced green onion (1)
- 2 teaspoons snipped fresh thyme
- $\frac{1}{2}$ teaspoon lower-sodium seafood seasoning*
- $\frac{1}{4}$ teaspoon black pepper
- $\frac{1}{3}$ cup whole wheat panko (Japanese-style bread crumbs)
- 2 teaspoons canola oil
- $\frac{1}{2}$ teaspoon finely shredded lemon peel

PER SERVING: 107 cal., 3 g total fat (1 g sat. fat), 49 mg chol., 246 mg sodium, 8 g carb. (1 g fiber, 1 g sugars), 11 g pro. Exchanges: 0.5 starch, 1.5 lean meat, 0.5 fat.

1 Preheat the oven to 450°F. Coat a 15x10x1-inch baking pan with cooking spray. Measure thickness of fish; pat fish dry with paper towels. Arrange the fish in a single layer in the prepared pan. Tuck under any thin edges. Bake, uncovered, for 4 to 6 minutes per $\frac{1}{2}$-inch thickness of fish or until fish flakes easily when tested with a fork. Remove fish from oven. Using a fork, coarsely flake fish. Set aside to cool.

2 In a medium bowl combine egg, soft bread crumbs, 3 tablespoons of the yogurt, green onion, thyme, seafood seasoning, and pepper. Stir in flaked fish.

3 Wipe the 15x10x1-inch baking pan clean and line with foil; coat foil with cooking spray. Spoon $\frac{1}{4}$-cup mounds of fish mixture onto baking pan about 2 inches apart. Pat and shape into 2- to $2\frac{1}{2}$-inch patties. In a small bowl combine the panko and canola oil. Carefully place each patty into panko mixture, turning to coat both sides. Return to baking pan, reshaping as necessary.

4 Bake, uncovered, for 12 to 15 minutes or until lightly browned and heated through (160°F). Stir lemon peel into remaining yogurt. Serve sole cakes with yogurt mixture.

*TEST KITCHEN TIP: Check the label for seafood seasoning that has 100 mg sodium or less per $\frac{1}{4}$ teaspoon.

Shrimp and Tomato Shooters

If tall shot glasses aren't part of your barware selection, look for plastic disposable ones where party supplies are sold.

SERVINGS 24 (1 shrimp and $3^1/_2$ ounces tomato mixture each)
CARB. PER SERVING 4 g
PREP 25 minutes
SLOW COOK 5 hours (low) or $2^1/_2$ hours (high) + 30 minutes (high)

2	28-ounce cans no-salt-added whole tomatoes, undrained, cut up
1	14.5-ounce can reduced-sodium chicken broth
1	cup seafood stock or clam juice
$^1/_2$	cup sliced leeks
$^1/_2$	cup chopped celery
$^1/_2$	cup chopped carrot
2	tablespoons no-salt-added tomato paste
2	bay leaves
2	cloves garlic, minced
$^1/_2$	teaspoon salt
$^1/_4$	teaspoon black pepper
$^1/_4$	cup evaporated fat-free milk
$^1/_2$	teaspoon snipped fresh thyme
2	tablespoons dry sherry (optional)
24	cooked, peeled, and deveined medium shrimp (about 12 ounces)
	Snipped fresh chives, celery leaves, or small basil leaves (optional)

PER SERVING: 38 cal., 0 g total fat, 30 mg chol., 266 mg sodium, 4 g carb. (1 g fiber, 2 g sugars), 4 g pro. Exchanges: 1 vegetable.

1 In a 5- to 6-quart slow cooker combine tomatoes, chicken broth, seafood stock, leeks, celery, carrot, tomato paste, bay leaves, garlic, salt, and pepper. Cover; cook on low-heat setting for 5 to 6 hours or on high-heat setting for $2^1/_2$ to 3 hours.

2 Stir in evaporated milk and thyme; if desired, stir in sherry. If using low-heat setting, turn to high-heat setting. Cover; cook for 30 minutes more.

3 Blend tomato mixture directly in the slow cooker until smooth using an immersion blender. (Or blend batches in a blender or food processor until smooth and return to slow cooker.)

4 To serve, divide tomato mixture among 24 tall shot glasses. Top each glass with a whole shrimp. If desired, sprinkle with snipped chives or garnish with celery or basil leaves.

Oven-Fried Zucchini Fries with Herbed Buttermilk Dipping Sauce

Baking these triple-dipped chubby fries in a hot oven instead of frying them in hot oil keeps the fat at just 1 gram per serving.

SERVINGS 8 (6 to 7 zucchini sticks and about 2$^1/_2$ tablespoons dip each)
CARB. PER SERVING 15 g
PREP 30 minutes
BAKE 14 minutes

Nonstick cooking spray

$^1/_2$ cup whole wheat flour

1$^1/_4$ pounds zucchini, cut into 3x$^1/_2$-inch sticks

2 egg whites, lightly beaten

$^1/_4$ cup low-fat buttermilk

$^1/_2$ cup fine dry whole wheat bread crumbs

1 tablespoon salt-free seasoning blend, such as Mrs. Dash Original brand

1 recipe Herbed Buttermilk Dipping Sauce

PER SERVING: 94 cal., 1 g total fat (0 g sat. fat), 1 mg chol., 123 mg sodium, 15 g carb. (2 g fiber, 5 g sugars), 6 g pro. Exchanges: 1 vegetable, 0.5 starch, 0.5 lean meat.

1 Preheat oven to 450°F. Line a large baking sheet with foil. Coat foil with cooking spray; set aside.

2 In a resealable plastic bag place $^1/_4$ cup of the whole wheat flour. Add the zucchini to the bag; seal bag and toss to coat. Remove zucchini from the bag.

3 In a shallow dish combine egg whites and the $^1/_4$ cup buttermilk. In a small bowl combine the remaining $^1/_4$ cup whole wheat flour, bread crumbs, and seasoning blend.

4 Working in batches, place one-fourth of the bread crumb mixture in the previously used resealable plastic bag. Dip one-fourth of the zucchini sticks in egg white mixture; drain off excess mixture. Transfer zucchini to bread crumb mixture in bag, seal bag and toss until all sides of the sticks are coated with bread crumb mixture. Remove coated zucchini from the bag. Add another one-fourth of the bread crumb mixture to bag along with one-fourth more of the zucchini. Continue until all of the zucchini has been coated. Arrange prepared zucchini fries in a single layer on prepared baking sheet. Coat zucchini fries with cooking spray.

5 Bake on the center rack of the oven for 7 minutes. Turn the zucchini fries and coat with cooking spray. Bake about 7 minutes more or until coating is crisp and golden and zucchini is just tender.

6 Serve warm zucchini fries with Herbed Buttermilk Dipping Sauce.

HERBED BUTTERMILK DIPPING SAUCE: In a small bowl combine one 6-ounce carton plain fat-free yogurt and $^1/_3$ cup low-fat buttermilk. Stir in 2 tablespoons snipped fresh chives; 1 tablespoon snipped fresh parsley; 2 teaspoons snipped fresh dill weed; 2 cloves garlic, minced; $^1/_2$ teaspoon onion powder; $^1/_4$ teaspoon black pepper; and pinch cayenne pepper.

Fennel-Mushroom Bruschetta

To prepare the fresh fennel, trim off both ends of the bulb, peel away any wilted layers, cut the bulb in half, and then cut into slices.

SERVINGS 12 (2 baguette slices and about 2 tablespoons topper each)
CARB. PER SERVING 15 g
PREP 10 minutes
COOK 12 minutes

1 tablespoon butter

1 small fennel bulb, thinly sliced

¼ of a medium sweet onion, chopped

1 8-ounce package sliced fresh mushrooms

2 cloves garlic, minced

2 tablespoons white wine or 1½ tablespoons reduced-sodium chicken broth plus 1½ teaspoons white wine vinegar

1 cup arugula

1 tablespoon reduced-sodium soy sauce

12 ounces whole wheat baguette-style French bread, cut into 24 thin slices, toasted

1 In a large skillet heat butter over medium heat. Add fennel and onion. Cook and stir about 5 minutes or until vegetables just begin to soften. Add mushrooms and garlic. Cook and stir for 3 to 5 minutes more or until vegetables are crisp-tender. Remove from heat. Carefully add wine to skillet. Return to heat. Cook and stir until nearly all of the liquid has evaporated, making sure to scrape up any browned bits from the bottom of the pan.

2 Remove pan from heat. Stir in arugula and soy sauce. Spoon about 1 tablespoon mushroom mixture over each toasted baguette slice.

PER SERVING: 93 cal., 2 g total fat (1 g sat. fat), 3 mg chol., 185 mg sodium, 15 g carb. (2 g fiber, 2 g sugars), 3 g pro. Exchanges: 1 starch, 0.5 fat.

2 grams fat

Broccoli Dill Dip with Sweet Potato Chips

Check out the health food section of the grocery store for the sweet potato chips. If they aren't there, they may be in the chip section.

SERVINGS 16 (2 tablespoons dip and ½ ounce potato chips each)
CARB. PER SERVING 10 g
PREP 20 minutes

- 1 teaspoon canola oil
- ½ cup finely chopped onion
- 2 cloves garlic, minced
- 4 ounces reduced-fat cream cheese (Neufchâtel), softened and cut up
- 1 cup plain fat-free yogurt
- 2 cups broccoli, blanched* and chopped
- 1 tablespoon snipped fresh dill weed
- 2 slices lower-sodium, lower-fat bacon or turkey bacon, crisp-cooked and crumbled

Fresh dill sprigs (optional)

- 8 ounces no-salt-added sweet potato chips, such as Terra brand

10 grams carb

PER SERVING: 118 cal., 8 g total fat (2 g sat. fat), 6 mg chol., 53 mg sodium, 10 g carb. (2 g fiber, 3 g sugars), 3 g pro. Exchanges: 2 vegetable, 1.5 fat.

1 In a small skillet heat oil over medium-high heat. Add onion and garlic. Cook and stir for 5 to 6 minutes or until onion is tender.

2 In a medium bowl beat cream cheese with an electric mixer on medium speed until light and fluffy. Beat in yogurt. Stir in broccoli, snipped dill, and onion mixture. Serve immediately or cover and chill up to 24 hours.

3 Stir in bacon just before serving. If desired, garnish with fresh dill sprigs. Serve with the sweet potato chips.

*TEST KITCHEN TIP: To blanch broccoli, place broccoli in a pot of boiling water; cook for 4 to 5 minutes. Remove broccoli with a slotted spoon and plunge into a bowl of ice water; drain and chop.

Roasted Red Pepper and Spinach Dip

A small slow cooker comes in handy for making creamy dips and other appetizers. The cooker should be at least half full, so do not substitute a larger size.

SERVINGS 16 (3 tablespoons dip and 6 tortilla wedges each)
CARB. PER SERVING 11 g
PREP 25 minutes
BAKE 12 minutes per batch
SLOW COOK 3 hours (low) or 1½ hours (high)

- 1 10-ounce package frozen chopped spinach, thawed
- 1½ cups bottled roasted red sweet peppers, drained and cut into ¼-inch strips
- 6 ounces fat-free cream cheese, softened
- 1½ cups shredded part-skim mozzarella cheese (6 ounces)
- 4 ounces smoked mozzarella cheese, shredded (1 cup)
- 2 tablespoons bottled minced garlic (12 cloves)
- 12 6-inch corn tortillas
- Nonstick cooking spray
- 2 tablespoons finely shredded Parmesan cheese

1 Squeeze out as much liquid as possible from the spinach. Pat roasted sweet peppers dry with paper towels.

2 In a 2-quart slow cooker stir together drained spinach, roasted sweet peppers, cream cheese, part-skim mozzarella cheese, smoked mozzarella cheese, and garlic. Cover; cook on low-heat setting about 3 hours or on high-heat setting for 1½ to 2 hours or until cheeses are melted and smooth.

3 Meanwhile, preheat oven to 375°F. Cut each tortilla into eight wedges, making 96 wedges total. Arrange tortilla wedges in a single layer on three large baking sheets. Coat wedges with cooking spray. Bake, one sheet at a time, about 12 minutes or until wedges are crisp and golden brown on edges. Set aside. (Do not bake more than one pan at a time or tortillas will not crisp properly.)

4 Sprinkle spinach mixture with Parmesan cheese. Serve with baked tortilla wedges.

PER SERVING: 111 cal., 4 g total fat (2 g sat. fat), 14 mg chol., 239 mg sodium, 11 g carb. (2 g fiber, 1 g sugars), 8 g pro. Exchanges: 0.5 starch, 1 lean meat, 0.5 fat.

Baba Ghanoush

Roasting helps intensify the mild flavor of eggplant. Once it's roasted, use a knife to peel away the skin or a serving spoon to scoop out the eggplant meat.

SERVINGS 16 (2 tablespoons dip and $1/2$ of a pita [3 to 4 wedges] each)
CARB. PER SERVING 21 g
PREP 15 minutes
GRILL 16 minutes

1 large eggplant, halved lengthwise
2 tablespoons olive oil
3 tablespoons lemon juice
2 tablespoons tahini (sesame seed paste)
3 cloves garlic
1/4 teaspoon salt
1/4 teaspoon ground cumin
1/4 teaspoon black pepper
1 tablespoon snipped fresh parsley
1/8 teaspoon smoked paprika
8 whole wheat pita bread rounds

PER SERVING: 124 cal., 4 g total fat (1 g sat. fat), 0 mg chol., 180 mg sodium, 21 g carb. (4 g fiber, 2 g sugars), 4 g pro. **Exchanges:** 1 vegetable, 1 starch, 1 fat.

1 Prick eggplant with a fork several times. Brush eggplant with 1 tablespoon of the olive oil.

2 For a charcoal grill, place eggplant on the grill rack directly over medium coals. Grill, covered, for 16 to 20 minutes or until tender and browned, turning once halfway through grilling. (For a gas grill, preheat grill. Reduce heat to medium. Place eggplant on grill rack over heat. Cover and grill as above.)

3 Allow eggplant to cool slightly. When cool enough to handle, peel eggplant or scoop out flesh from peel using a spoon. For dip, transfer eggplant flesh to a food processor. Add the remaining 1 tablespoon olive oil, the lemon juice, tahini, garlic, salt, cumin, and pepper. Cover and process until nearly smooth.

4 Transfer to a serving dish. Sprinkle with parsley and paprika. If desired, warm the pita bread rounds. Cut each pita bread round into 6 to 8 wedges. Serve dip with the pita wedges.

Caramelized Onion and Swiss Dip

Cut the cream cheese into small cubes so it's easy to mix into the onion-broth mixture and will melt evenly.

SERVINGS 24 (2 tablespoons dip and 8 vegetable dippers each)
CARB. PER SERVING 7 g
PREP 25 minutes
SLOW COOK 6 hours (low) or 3 hours (high) + 45 minutes (low)

4½ cups chopped onions (about 4 large)

¼ cup lower-sodium beef broth or reduced-sodium chicken broth

¼ cup dry white wine

2 tablespoons butter

1 large clove garlic, minced

¼ teaspoon black pepper

6 ounces reduced-fat cream cheese (Neufchâtel), cut up

2 cups shredded Swiss cheese (8 ounces)

2 tablespoons flour

Black pepper (optional)

Sliced carrot sticks, celery sticks, sweet pepper strips, endive leaves, and/or broccoli florets

PER SERVING: 91 cal., 5 g total fat (3 g sat. fat), 16 mg chol., 74 mg sodium, 7 g carb. (1 g fiber, 2 g sugars), 4 g pro. Exchanges: 2 vegetable, 1 fat.

1 In a 2-quart slow cooker combine onions, broth, wine, butter, garlic, and the ¼ teaspoon black pepper. Cover; cook on low-heat setting for 6 to 7 hours or on high-heat setting for 3 to 3½ hours. If using high-heat setting, reduce cooker to low-heat setting. Add cream cheese, stirring until combined.

2 In a medium bowl combine Swiss cheese and flour. Stir into the mixture in the slow cooker. Cover; cook on low-heat setting for 45 minutes to 1 hour more or until all of the cheese is melted and mixture is heated through.

3 If desired, sprinkle dip with additional black pepper. Serve with vegetables for dipping.

Red and Green Layered Bean Dip

Bottled salsa is typically high in sodium, so we created our own lower-sodium red and green varieties.

SERVINGS 24 ($^1/_4$ cup dip and $^3/_4$ ounce baked tortilla chips each)
CARB. PER SERVING 21 g
PREP 30 minutes
GRILL 10 minutes

1   15-ounce can reduced-sodium refried beans, such as Amy's brand

1   recipe Red Salsa

1   cup plain fat-free Greek yogurt

2   teaspoons chili powder

1   recipe Green Salsa

1   cup canned no-salt-added black beans, rinsed and drained

$^1/_3$ cup sliced green onions (2 or 3)

$^1/_3$ cup crumbled queso fresco

1   tablespoon coarsely chopped fresh cilantro

18   ounces baked tortilla chips

1 In a 2-quart baking dish spread refried beans. Top with Red Salsa. In a small bowl combine Greek yogurt and chili powder. Spread mixture over Red Salsa in dish. Top with Green Salsa. Sprinkle with black beans, green onions, queso fresco, and cilantro. Serve immediately or cover and chill for up to 24 hours. Serve with baked tortilla chips.

RED SALSA: In a medium bowl combine 1 cup seeded and chopped tomatoes; $^1/_2$ cup chopped red sweet pepper; $^1/_2$ cup chopped red onion; 1 small red hot chile pepper, seeded and finely chopped (see tip, *page 33);* 1 tablespoon lemon juice; 1 clove garlic, minced; $^1/_2$ teaspoon chili powder; $^1/_4$ teaspoon ground cumin; $^1/_4$ teaspoon paprika; and $^1/_4$ teaspoon black pepper.

GREEN SALSA: Husk and rinse 12 ounces tomatillos (8 tomatillos). Cut 1 small onion into $^1/_2$-inch-thick slices. Halve and remove seeds from 2 fresh jalapeño chile peppers (see tip, *page 33).* Brush tomatillos, onion slices, and jalapeño halves with 1 tablespoon olive oil. For a charcoal or gas grill, place tomatillos, onion slices, and jalapeño peppers on the grill rack directly over medium heat. Grill, covered, for 10 to 15 minutes or until softened and darkened, turning once halfway through grilling. (To broil, preheat broiler. Place tomatillos, onion slices, and jalapeño peppers on a broiler pan. Broil 4 to 5 inches from the heat for 8 to 10 minutes or until skins are softened and darkened, turning once.) Cool vegetables slightly. Transfer to a food processor. Add $^1/_4$ cup fresh cilantro leaves, 1 tablespoon lime juice, 2 cloves garlic, $^1/_4$ teaspoon salt, and $^1/_4$ teaspoon black pepper. Cover and process until nearly smooth.

5 grams protein

PER SERVING: 161 cal., 7 g total fat (1 g sat. fat), 1 mg chol., 162 mg sodium, 21 g carb. (4 g fiber, 2 g sugars), 5 g pro. Exchanges: 1.5 starch, 1 fat.

3

comforting
soups and stews

There's something satisfying about a steaming bowl of soup,

and these good-for-you recipes will not disappoint. Colorful and

comforting, each meal in a bowl cuts calories, fat, and carbs,

making them perfect partners in your meal plan.

Pork and Poblano Stew

Hot chili powder gives this quick stew a spicy kick. If you like
your foods on the mild side, use regular chili powder instead.

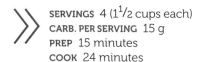

SERVINGS 4 (1$\frac{1}{2}$ cups each)
CARB. PER SERVING 15 g
PREP 15 minutes
COOK 24 minutes

1$\frac{1}{4}$ pounds pork tenderloin, cut into $\frac{3}{4}$- to 1-inch pieces

2 teaspoons hot chili powder

2 tablespoons olive oil

1 fresh poblano chile pepper, seeded and cut into 1 inch pieces (see tip, *page 33*)

1 large red sweet pepper, cut into 1-inch pieces

1 medium onion, cut into thin wedges

1 14.5-ounce can fire-roasted tomatoes with garlic, undrained

1 14.5-ounce can reduced-sodium chicken broth

3 inches stick cinnamon

2 teaspoons finely shredded orange peel (set aside)

$\frac{1}{4}$ cup fresh orange juice

1 | Toss pork with chili powder to coat. In a large saucepan heat 1 tablespoon of the oil over medium-high heat. Cook the pork about 4 minutes or until browned, stirring occasionally. Using a slotted spoon, remove pork from pan; set aside.

2 | Add remaining oil to the saucepan. Add poblano pepper, sweet pepper, and onion; cook over medium-high heat until vegetables are just tender, about 5 minutes. Add tomatoes, broth, and cinnamon stick. Bring to boiling; reduce heat. Simmer, covered, over medium-low heat for 10 minutes. Add reserved pork and orange juice. Simmer, uncovered, about 5 minutes more or until pork is done. Stir in orange peel.

3 | To serve, remove stick cinnamon and ladle stew into four shallow serving bowls.

15 grams carb

PER SERVING: 295 cal., 11 g total fat (2 g sat. fat), 87 mg chol., 534 mg sodium, 15 g carb. (4 g fiber, 7 g sugars), 32 g pro. Exchanges: 2 vegetable, 4 lean meat, 1.5 fat.

QUICK TIP
Save mealtime prep by cutting the pork, peppers, and onion ahead of time. Refrigerate meat and the veggies in separate covered containers until needed.

Sausage and Broccoli Rabe Soup

Broccoli rabe, also known as rapini, is related to cabbage and turnips.

SERVINGS 6 (1⅓ cups each)
CARB. PER SERVING 19 g
START TO FINISH 35 minutes

Nonstick cooking spray

8 ounces smoked turkey sausage, chopped

1 medium red sweet pepper, cut into thin bite-size strips

2 medium shallots, thinly sliced

4 cups water

1 cup reduced-sodium chicken broth

2 cups cauliflower florets

2 cups coarsely chopped, trimmed broccoli rabe, Swiss chard, or kale (5 ounces)

1 15-ounce can no-salt-added cannellini beans, rinsed and drained

1 tablespoon snipped fresh oregano or 1 teaspoon dried oregano, crushed

¼ teaspoon crushed red pepper (optional)

2 tablespoons balsamic vinegar or red wine vinegar

1 ounce Parmesan cheese, shaved

PER SERVING: 186 cal., 6 g total fat (2 g sat. fat), 33 mg chol., 606 mg sodium, 19 g carb. (5 g fiber, 4 g sugars), 14 g pro. Exchanges: 1 vegetable, 1 starch, 1.5 lean meat, 0.5 fat.

1 Coat an unheated 4- to 5-quart Dutch oven with cooking spray; heat over medium-high heat. Add sausage, sweet pepper, and shallots. Cook about 5 minutes or until sausage is lightly browned, stirring occasionally.

2 Add water, broth, cauliflower, broccoli rabe, cannellini beans, dried oregano (if using), and, if desired, crushed red pepper. Bring to boiling; reduce heat. Simmer, covered, for 5 to 7 minutes or until cauliflower and broccoli rabe stems are tender.

3 Stir in vinegar and fresh oregano (if using). To serve, ladle soup into six serving bowls and garnish with shaved Parmesan cheese.

Curried Turkey Stew with Toasted Naan

Yellow curry paste, often used in Thai cuisine, is milder than the red variety. Look for curry paste at Asian food markets.

SERVINGS 6 (1$\frac{1}{3}$ cups stew and $\frac{1}{3}$ naan each)
CARB. PER SERVING 32 g
PREP 35 minutes
COOK 25 minutes
BROIL 2 minutes

- 1$\frac{1}{2}$ pounds turkey breast tenderloins, cut into thin bite-size strips
- 2 teaspoons ground coriander
- 1 teaspoon ground cumin
- $\frac{1}{2}$ teaspoon ground ginger
- $\frac{1}{4}$ teaspoon black pepper
- 1 tablespoon canola oil
- Nonstick cooking spray
- 2 medium carrots, thinly sliced
- 1 medium onion, chopped
- 1 stalk celery, thinly sliced
- 3 cups water
- 2 cups cauliflower florets
- 1 cup coarsely chopped, trimmed fresh kale or spinach
- 1 cup reduced-sodium chicken broth
- $\frac{1}{4}$ cup flour
- 1 to 2 tablespoons yellow or red curry paste
- 1 cup fresh snow pea pods, trimmed and halved lengthwise
- 2 wheat or whole grain naan breads (about 8 ounces total)

PER SERVING: 309 cal., 5 g total fat (0 g sat. fat), 70 mg chol., 440 mg sodium, 32 g carb. (6 g fiber, 4 g sugars), 36 g pro. Exchanges: 1.5 vegetable, 1.5 starch, 4.5 lean meat, 0.5 fat.

1 Place turkey strips in a large bowl. In a small bowl combine coriander, cumin, ginger, and pepper. Sprinkle over turkey and toss to coat.

2 In a large saucepan heat oil over medium heat. Add half the turkey; cook until browned, stirring occasionally. Remove turkey from the pan and repeat with remaining turkey. Set all turkey aside.

3 Coat the saucepan with cooking spray if needed. Add carrots, onion, and celery to saucepan; cook over medium heat for 5 minutes, stirring occasionally. Add water, cauliflower, and kale. Bring to boiling; reduce heat. Simmer, covered, for 5 minutes.

4 In a small bowl whisk together broth, flour, and curry paste until smooth. Add to cauliflower mixture along with snow peas and browned turkey. Cook and stir until slightly thickened and bubbly. Cook and stir for 2 minutes more or until turkey is no longer pink and vegetables are just tender.

5 Meanwhile, cut each naan bread into three portions. Broil 4 to 5 inches from the heat for 2 to 3 minutes or until toasted, turning once halfway through broiling.

6 To serve, ladle stew into six serving bowls. Top each serving with a piece of toasted naan.

QUICK TIP
Use a wire whisk
when combining the
fat-free half-and-half
and the flour so the
mixture is lump-free
before adding it to
the soup.

Turkey and Sweet Potato Soup

Fat-free half-and-half adds creamy richness to this comforting soup while keeping the fat at just 5 grams.

SERVINGS 6 (1¼ cups each)
CARB. PER SERVING 14 g
PREP 20 minutes
COOK 20 minutes

3 slices bacon, chopped

½ of a medium red onion, cut into thin wedges (½ cup)

3 cloves garlic, minced

2½ cups water

1 14.5-ounce can reduced-sodium chicken broth

6 ounces sweet potato, peeled and cut into ½-inch cubes

1 medium zucchini (about 6 ounces), halved lengthwise and thinly sliced

1 tablespoon snipped fresh thyme or 1 teaspoon dried thyme, crushed

8 ounces roasted turkey breast, coarsely shredded (2 cups)

1 cup fat-free half-and-half

2 tablespoons flour

2 tablespoons Dijon-style mustard

1 In a 4-quart Dutch oven cook bacon until browned and crisp, stirring occasionally. Remove from pan and drain on paper towels. Reserve 1 tablespoon drippings in the Dutch oven.

2 Add onion and garlic to the pan drippings. Cook over medium heat for 3 to 5 minutes or until onion is just tender, stirring occasionally. Add water, broth, and sweet potato. Bring to boiling; reduce heat. Simmer, covered, for 5 minutes.

3 Add zucchini and dried thyme (if using). Return to boiling; reduce heat. Simmer, covered, about 5 minutes more or until potato and zucchini are tender. Add fresh thyme (if using) and the turkey. In a small bowl whisk together half-and-half and flour until smooth. Add to soup. Cook and stir until slightly thickened and bubbly. Cook and stir for 1 minute more. Stir in mustard.

4 To serve, ladle soup into six serving bowls. Sprinkle with cooked bacon.

PER SERVING: 164 cal., 5 g total fat (2 g sat. fat), 39 mg chol., 435 mg sodium, 14 g carb. (1 g fiber, 5 g sugars), 16 g pro. Exchanges: 1 starch, 2 lean meat, 0.5 fat.

5 grams fat

Barbecue Meatball Soup

An instant-read thermometer works best for checking the doneness of the meatballs' doneness, but if don't have one, cut a meatball open to make sure the center is no longer pink.

SERVINGS 6 (1⅓ cups each)
CARB. PER SERVING 14 g
PREP 25 minutes
BAKE 15 minutes
COOK 20 minutes

¾ cup soft whole wheat bread crumbs

¼ cup refrigerated or frozen egg product, thawed, or 1 egg, lightly beaten

3 cloves garlic, minced

¼ teaspoon black pepper

¼ teaspoon smoked paprika or sweet paprika

1 pound 90% lean ground beef

2 medium carrots, thinly sliced

2 stalks celery, thinly sliced

2 medium red, yellow, and/or green sweet peppers, cut into thin bite-size strips

1 medium onion, chopped

1 tablespoon canola oil

3 cups water

1 cup lower-sodium beef broth

½ cup light barbecue sauce

3 cups coarsely chopped, trimmed collard greens, mustard, greens, or kale

½ cup crumbled reduced-fat blue cheese (2 ounces)

PER SERVING: 243 cal., 11 g total fat (4 g sat. fat), 53 mg chol., 540 mg sodium, 14 g carb. (3 g fiber, 6 g sugars), 21 g pro. Exchanges: 2 vegetable, 2.5 medium-fat meat, 0.5 fat.

1 Preheat oven to 350°F. For meatballs, in a large bowl combine bread crumbs, egg, garlic, black pepper, and paprika. Add ground beef; mix well. Shape meat mixture into twenty-four 1-inch meatballs. Place meatballs in a foil-lined 13×9×2-inch baking pan. Bake about 15 minutes or until done in centers (160°F). Set aside.

2 Meanwhile, in a 4- to 5-quart Dutch oven cook carrots, celery, sweet peppers, and onion in hot oil over medium heat for 5 minutes, stirring occasionally. Add water, broth, and barbecue sauce. Bring to boiling. Add collard greens. Return to boiling; reduce heat. Simmer, uncovered, for 5 to 7 minutes or until vegetables are tender.

3 Add cooked meatballs to soup; heat through. To serve, ladle soup into six serving bowls and sprinkle with blue cheese.

Beef Stew with Garlic-Thyme Sour Cream

On a day when you need a fuss-free meal, pull out your slow cooker in the morning to get this hearty classic started for an all-day simmer.

>> SERVINGS 8 (1^1/$_2$ cups stew and about 1^1/$_2$ tablespoons topping each)
CARB. PER SERVING 21 g
PREP 30 minutes
SLOW COOK 8 hours (low) or 4 hours (high)

2 pounds boneless beef arm pot roast, trimmed of fat and cut into 1-inch pieces

1 tablespoon canola oil

2 cups halved cremini or button mushrooms

4 medium carrots, cut into 1-inch pieces

1 pound round red potatoes, cut into 1-inch pieces

2 medium parsnips, cut into 1-inch pieces

2 stalks celery, cut into 1-inch pieces

1 cup frozen pearl onions

3 cloves garlic, minced

1 tablespoon snipped fresh rosemary or 1^1/$_2$ teaspoons dried rosemary, crushed

4 cups lower-sodium beef broth

^{1}/$_3$ cup red wine or pomegranate juice

^{3}/$_4$ cup light sour cream

1 clove garlic, minced

2 teaspoons snipped fresh thyme

PER SERVING: 289 cal., 9 g total fat (3 g sat. fat), 80 mg chol., 342 mg sodium, 21 g carb. (3 g fiber, 5 g sugars), 30 g pro. Exchanges: 1 vegetable, 1 starch, 3.5 lean meat, 0.5 fat.

1 In a large skillet brown meat on all sides, half at a time, in hot oil over medium heat. Using a slotted spoon, transfer meat to a 5- to 6-quart slow cooker. Add mushrooms, carrots, potatoes, parsnips, celery, onions, 3 minced cloves garlic, and rosemary. Pour broth over all.

2 Cover and cook on low-heat setting for 8 to 10 hours or on high-heat setting for 4 to 5 hours. Stir in wine just before serving.

3 For topping, in a small bowl stir together sour cream, 1 minced clove garlic, and thyme. To serve, ladle stew into eight serving bowls. Top each serving with some of the sour cream mixture.

Mole Chicken Chili

Look for bottled mole sauce with the Mexican ingredients in the grocery store or take a trip to a Mexican food market.

SERVINGS 6 (1½ cups each)
CARB. PER SERVING 32 g
PREP 25 minutes
COOK 30 minutes

2 teaspoons unsweetened cocoa powder

1½ teaspoons ground ancho chile pepper or paprika

1 teaspoon ground cumin

½ teaspoon salt

1½ pounds skinless boneless chicken breast halves, cut into 1-inch pieces

Nonstick cooking spray

2 medium red and/or green sweet peppers, cut into thin bite-size strips

1 large onion, chopped (1 cup)

1 fresh jalapeño chile pepper, finely chopped* (optional)

1 tablespoon canola oil

2 14.5-ounce cans no-salt-added diced tomatoes, undrained

1 15-ounce can reduced-sodium black beans, rinsed and drained

1 cup frozen whole kernel corn

½ cup hot water

2 tablespoons bottled mole sauce

½ cup light sour cream (optional)

¼ cup snipped fresh cilantro

Lime wedges

1 In a small bowl combine cocoa powder, ancho pepper, cumin, and salt. Place chicken pieces in a large bowl. Sprinkle with cocoa powder mixture; toss to coat. Coat an unheated nonstick Dutch oven with cooking spray; heat over medium-high heat. Add half the chicken pieces and cook until browned, stirring occasionally. Transfer chicken to a bowl and repeat with remaining half of chicken. Set chicken aside.

2 In the same Dutch oven cook sweet peppers, onion, and, if desired, jalapeño pepper in hot oil over medium heat about 5 minutes or until tender, stirring occasionally. Add tomatoes, black beans, corn, and browned chicken. In a small bowl combine water and mole sauce until smooth. Add to chicken mixture. Bring to boiling; reduce heat. Simmer, covered, for 20 minutes to cook chicken and blend flavors.

3 To serve, ladle chili into six serving bowls. If desired, top with sour cream. Sprinkle with cilantro and serve with lime wedges.

SLOW COOKER DIRECTIONS: Prepare as directed through Step 1. In a 4- to 5-quart slow cooker combine browned chicken, sweet peppers, onion, and jalapeño pepper (if using). Omit the canola oil. Add diced tomatoes, black beans, and corn. In a small bowl combine water and mole sauce until smooth. Add to slow cooker. Cover and cook on low-heat setting for 4 to 5 hours or on high-heat setting for 2 to 2½ hours. Serve as directed.

***TEST KITCHEN TIP:** Because hot chile peppers contain volatile oils that can burn your skin and eyes, avoid direct contact with them as much as possible. When working with chile peppers, wear plastic or rubber gloves. If your bare hands do touch the peppers, wash your hands and nails well with soap and warm water.

7 grams fat

PER SERVING: 297 cal., 7 g total fat (1 g sat. fat), 73 mg chol., 526 mg sodium, 32 g carb. (8 g fiber, 8 g sugars), 31 g pro. Exchanges: 2 vegetable, 1.5 starch, 2 lean meat, 0.5 fat.

Roasted Garlic Sunchoke and Potato Soup

Sunchokes, also known as Jerusalem artichokes, have nothing to do with Jerusalem or artichokes. They are a knobby tuberous root with a delicate, nutty flavor.

SERVINGS 4 (1$\frac{1}{2}$ cups each)
CARB. PER SERVING 38 g
PREP 30 minutes
ROAST 25 minutes
COOK 25 minutes

- 1 large fennel bulb
- 1 large onion
- 1 bulb garlic
- 1 tablespoon olive oil
- 3 cups low-sodium vegetable broth
- 2 cups cubed, peeled potatoes (about 2 medium)
- 1$\frac{1}{2}$ cups cubed, peeled sunchokes (Jerusalem artichokes)
- $\frac{1}{2}$ teaspoon salt
- 1 miniature red sweet pepper, very thinly sliced crosswise, or $\frac{1}{2}$ cup very thin 1-inch strips red sweet pepper
- Coarsely ground black pepper

PER SERVING: 196 cal., 4 g total fat (1 g sat. fat), 0 mg chol., 446 mg sodium, 38 g carb. (6 g fiber, 10 g sugars), 5 g pro. Exchanges: 1 vegetable, 2 starch, 0.5 fat.

1 Preheat oven to 425°F. Trim tops off fennel bulb, reserving some of the green feathery fronds for a garnish. Cut a thin slice off the bottom of the bulb and cut out the core from the fennel bulb. Cut fennel bulb into thin wedges. Cut onion into thin wedges. Combine fennel and onion in a shallow roasting pan.

2 Peel away the dry outer layers of skin from the bulb of garlic, leaving skins and cloves intact. Cut off the pointed top portion (about $\frac{1}{4}$ inch), leaving bulb intact but exposing the individual cloves. Place the garlic bulb, cut side up, in a custard cup. Drizzle with about $\frac{1}{2}$ teaspoon of the olive oil. Drizzle remaining olive oil over onion and fennel wedges; toss to coat. Cover cup containing garlic with foil. Roast onion mixture and garlic for 25 to 35 minutes or until vegetables are tender and lightly browned and the garlic cloves feel soft when pressed, stirring vegetable mixture once halfway through roasting.

3 Meanwhile, in a large saucepan combine broth, potatoes, sunchokes, and salt. Bring to boiling; reduce heat. Simmer, covered, about 20 minutes or until vegetables are very tender. Remove from heat and cool slightly.

4 Set garlic aside just until cool enough to handle. Squeeze out the garlic paste from individual cloves into a blender or food processor. Add half of the roasted vegetables and half of the undrained potato mixture. Cover and blend or process until smooth. Repeat with remaining roasted vegetables and remaining undrained potato mixture. Combine all pureed mixture in a large saucepan. Cook over medium heat just until heated through, stirring frequently.

5 To serve, ladle soup into four serving bowls. Chop reserved fennel fronds and sprinkle over soup. Garnish with sliced sweet pepper and black pepper.

Coconut Squash Soup with Seared Scallops

To get the caramelized browning on the scallops, it's important to heat the grill pan or skillet before adding the sweet sea gems.

SERVINGS 4 (1$\frac{1}{2}$ cups soup and 2 scallops each)
CARB. PER SERVING 39 g
START TO FINISH 1 hour 15 minutes

8   medium fresh or frozen sea scallops (8 to 9 ounces)

Nonstick cooking spray

2   medium leeks, trimmed and thinly sliced

3   cloves garlic, minced

2   teaspoons grated fresh ginger

2   cups low-sodium vegetable broth

1   2-pound butternut squash, peeled and cut into 1-inch pieces (6 cups)

1   14-ounce can reduced-fat unsweetened coconut milk

$\frac{1}{8}$ teaspoon cayenne pepper

$\frac{1}{2}$ teaspoon ground coriander

$\frac{1}{8}$ teaspoon salt

$\frac{1}{8}$ teaspoon black pepper

$\frac{1}{4}$ cup pumpkin seeds (pepitas), toasted (optional)

2   tablespoons snipped fresh cilantro

2   teaspoons finely shredded lime peel (optional)

PER SERVING: 234 cal., 6 g total fat (4 g sat. fat), 14 mg chol., 614 mg sodium, 39 g carb. (5 g fiber, 7 g sugars), 10 g pro. Exchanges: 1 vegetable, 2 starch, 1 lean meat, 0.5 fat.

1 Thaw scallops, if frozen. Rinse scallops and pat dry with paper towels; set aside.

2 Coat an unheated large saucepan with cooking spray; heat pan over medium heat. Add leeks. Cook for 3 minutes, stirring occasionally. Add garlic and ginger. Cook and stir for 1 minute more.

3 Add broth and squash to leek mixture. Bring to boiling; reduce heat. Simmer, covered, about 15 minutes or until squash is tender. Remove from the heat and cool slightly.

4 Transfer squash mixture to a blender or food processor. Cover and blend or process until smooth. Return mixture to the saucepan. Stir in coconut milk and cayenne pepper. Heat through over medium-low heat, stirring occasionally (do not boil).

5 In a small bowl combine coriander, salt, and black pepper. Sprinkle evenly over scallops. Coat an unheated indoor grill pan or large nonstick skillet with cooking spray; heat over medium-high heat. Add scallops to hot grill pan or skillet. Cook for 3 to 4 minutes or until scallops are opaque, turning once halfway through cooking.

6 To serve, ladle soup into four serving bowls. Float 2 scallops on each serving of soup. Sprinkle with pumpkin seeds (if using), cilantro, and lime peel (if using).

Seafood Chowder with Lemon-Ginger Corn Croutons

Add a salad of fresh mixed greens, apple slices, thin onion wedges, and a light balsamic vinaigrette to complete this holiday-special soup.

SERVINGS 6 (1$\frac{1}{3}$ cups soup plus croutons each)
CARB. PER SERVING 24 g
PREP 25 minutes
COOK 20 minutes

- 6 ounces fresh or frozen peeled and deveined shrimp
- 6 ounces fresh or frozen skinless cod or halibut
- 1 recipe Lemon-Ginger Corn Croutons
- 1 large onion, halved and cut into thin wedges
- 1 tablespoon olive oil
- 3 cloves garlic, minced
- 3 cups water
- 1 14.5-ounce can reduced-sodium chicken broth
- 1 large rutabaga, peeled and cut into $\frac{1}{2}$-inch pieces (about 3 cups)
- 1$\frac{1}{2}$ cups frozen French-cut green beans
- 1 6-ounce can lump crabmeat, drained and cartilage removed
- $\frac{1}{2}$ cup bottled roasted red sweet peppers, drained and chopped

PER SERVING: 211 cal., 4 g total fat (1 g sat. fat), 85 mg chol., 442 mg sodium, 24 g carb. (4 g fiber, 7 g sugars), 20 g pro. Exchanges: 1 vegetable, 1 starch, 2 lean meat, 0.5 fat.

1 Thaw shrimp and cod, if frozen. Rinse shrimp and cod and pat dry with paper towels. Cut cod into 1-inch pieces. Set aside. Prepare Lemon-Ginger Corn Croutons.

2 In a large saucepan cook onion in hot oil over medium heat about 5 minutes or until tender, stirring occasionally. Add garlic; cook and stir for 1 minute. Add water, broth, and rutabaga. Bring to boiling; reduce heat. Simmer, covered, about 10 minutes or until rutabaga is tender. Remove from the heat and cool slightly.

3 Transfer half of the rutabaga mixture to a blender or food processor. Cover and blend or process until smooth; set aside.

4 Add green beans to remaining rutabaga mixture in saucepan; bring to boiling. Add shrimp and cod to the saucepan. Return to boiling; reduce heat. Simmer, covered, for 2 to 3 minutes or until shrimp are opaque and cod flakes when tested with a fork.

5 Add crab, roasted sweet pepper, and the pureed rutabaga mixture to the shrimp mixture in saucepan. Heat and stir over medium-low heat until heated through.

6 To serve, ladle chowder into six serving bowls. Top with Lemon-Ginger Corn Croutons just before serving.

LEMON-GINGER CORN CROUTONS: In a small bowl combine $\frac{1}{3}$ cup flour, $\frac{1}{4}$ cup yellow cornmeal, $\frac{1}{2}$ teaspoon baking powder, and $\frac{1}{4}$ teaspoon ground ginger. Make a well in the center of the flour mixture; set aside. In another bowl combine $\frac{1}{3}$ cup fat-free milk; 3 tablespoons light sour cream; 3 tablespoons refrigerated or frozen egg product, thawed; and 1$\frac{1}{2}$ teaspoons finely shredded lemon peel. Add all at once to flour mixture; stir just until moistened but still slightly lumpy. Drop batter in six even mounds onto a hot, lightly greased griddle, spreading mounds to about $\frac{1}{2}$ inch thick or make miniature cakes by dropping 1 tablespoon-size mounds onto the griddle. Cook over medium heat about 1 to 2 minutes on each side or until cakes are golden brown and edges are crisp, turning to second sides when cakes have bubbly surfaces and edges are slightly dry. Transfer larger cakes to a cutting board and cut into cubes. Transfer cubes or miniature cakes to a baking sheet. Keep warm in a 200°F oven.

main-dish
masterpieces

Embrace health-smart entertaining with festive entreés such as

a rolled pork roast with colorful, flavorful spirals and a dressed-

up turkey and maple-sauced pasta medley. Each one is special

enough to serve company, yet light enough to keep your daily

meal plan in check.

Bacon-Wrapped Pork Tenderloin and Roasted Vegetables

To wrap with bacon, start at one end of pork and carefully wrap a bacon slice around the tenderloin, adding another where one stops.

SERVINGS 4 (4 ounces pork, 1$\frac{1}{2}$ cups vegetables, and 1$\frac{1}{2}$ tablespoons pesto each)
CARB. PER SERVING 32 g
PREP 25 minutes
ROAST 25 minutes
STAND 3 minutes

2 tablespoons Dijon-style mustard

2 tablespoons honey

1 1-pound pork tenderloin

3 slices turkey bacon

12 ounces small red potatoes, scrubbed and quartered

6 cups cauliflower florets

$\frac{1}{4}$ teaspoon salt

$\frac{1}{4}$ teaspoon black pepper

$\frac{3}{4}$ cup packed fresh arugula, spinach, or sorrel (about 1$\frac{1}{2}$ ounces)

$\frac{1}{4}$ cup packed fresh Italian (flat-leaf) parsley

1 ounce Parmesan cheese, grated

2 tablespoons slivered almonds

1 clove garlic, minced

2 tablespoons olive oil

2 teaspoons lemon juice

1 to 2 tablespoons water

1 Preheat oven to 425°F. In a small bowl combine mustard and honey. Spread half of the mixture evenly over outside of pork. Wrap bacon around pork, leaving ends of bacon slices under the pork. Place pork on a rack in a large shallow roasting pan. Arrange potatoes and cauliflower around pork in pan. Drizzle with remaining mustard mixture. Toss vegetables to coat. Sprinkle potato mixture with the salt and pepper.

2 Roast for 25 to 30 minutes or until an instant-read thermometer inserted in thickest part of the pork registers 145°F and potatoes and cauliflower are just tender. Cover pork with foil and let stand for 3 minutes.

3 Meanwhile, for pesto, in a food processor place arugula, parsley, cheese, almonds, and garlic. Cover and process until finely chopped. With the processor running, add oil, lemon juice, and water through the feed tube until mixture is well combined.

4 To serve, cut pork crosswise into eight slices. Arrange pork and vegetables on a serving platter. Serve with pesto.

PER SERVING: 404 cal., 17 g total fat (4 g sat. fat), 84 mg chol., 726 mg sodium, 32 g carb. (5 g fiber, 13 g sugars), 33 g pro. Exchanges: 2 vegetable, 1 starch, 0.5 carb., 4 lean meat, 1.5 fat.

33 grams protein

Apricot-Stuffed Pork Tenderloin

Pork tenderloin is often sold vacuum-packed with two per package. Look for the weight on the label and choose a package that is around 3 pounds.

SERVINGS 12 (3 thin slices each and 1½ teaspoons preserves each)
CARB. PER SERVING 21 g
PREP 45 minutes
ROAST 50 minutes
STAND 10 minutes

- 4 slices white bread, torn
- 3 tablespoons butter, melted

Nonstick cooking spray

- 1 cup dried apricots
- ½ cup fresh Italian (flat-leaf) parsley leaves
- 2 teaspoons fresh thyme leaves
- 1 medium onion, cut up
- 1 stalk celery, cut up
- 2 tablespoons olive oil
- ½ cup reduced-sodium chicken broth
- ½ teaspoon salt
- ¼ teaspoon black pepper
- 2 1½-pound pork tenderloins

Salt

Black pepper

- ½ cup apricot preserves, melted

PER SERVING: 247 cal., 7 g total fat (3 g sat. fat), 77 mg chol., 291 mg sodium, 21 g carb. (1 g fiber, 13 g sugars), 24 g pro. Exchanges: 1 vegetable, 0.5 fruit, 0.5 carb., 3 lean meat, 1 fat.

1 Preheat oven to 375°F. Line a 15x10x1-inch baking pan with foil; set aside. For stuffing, place bread in a food processor. Cover and process until coarse crumbs form. Transfer to a large bowl. Drizzle with melted butter; toss to coat.

2 Spread crumbs evenly in the prepared baking pan. Bake for 6 to 8 minutes or until golden, stirring once. Return bread crumbs to the large bowl. Place a rack in the foil-lined baking pan and coat with cooking spray; set pan aside.

3 In the food processor combine dried apricots, parsley, and thyme. Cover and process with on/off pulses until finely chopped. Stir mixture into bread crumbs.

4 In the food processor combine onion and celery. Cover and process until finely chopped. In a small skillet cook onion and celery in hot oil over medium heat about 5 minutes or until tender. Stir in broth; cook for 1 minute. Add onion mixture, ½ teaspoon salt, and ¼ teaspoon pepper to bread mixture, stirring to moisten.

5 Trim fat from pork. Using a sharp knife, make a lengthwise cut down the center of a tenderloin, cutting to, but not through, the opposite side. Cut horizontally into the meat, slicing away from the center cut and cutting to, but not through, the opposite side. Repeat on the opposite side. Open so pork is flat. Repeat for other tenderloin. Place each tenderloin between two pieces of plastic wrap. Using the flat side of a meat mallet, pound each tenderloin lightly from center to edges into a 12x8-inch rectangle.

6 Spread stuffing over meat to within 1 inch of the edges. Starting from a short side, roll each rectangle into a spiral. Tie with 100-percent-cotton kitchen string. Place stuffed tenderloins, seam sides down, on the rack in the foil-lined baking pan. Sprinkle with additional salt and pepper (up to ¼ teaspoon each).

7 Roast, uncovered, for 50 to 55 minutes or until an instant-read thermometer inserted in the stuffing registers 145°F. Brush meat with 2 tablespoons of the preserves during the last 5 minutes of roasting. Remove from oven. Cover meat with foil and let stand for 10 minutes. Remove string from meat before slicing. Serve with the remaining preserves.

Lemon-Thyme Spiraled Pork Loin

If you don't have a meat mallet, use the bottom of a clean heavy saucepan to pound the meat to an even thickness.

SERVINGS 8 (3 ounces cooked pork each)
CARB. PER SERVING 1 g
PREP 45 minutes
ROAST 50 minutes
STAND 3 minutes

- 1 2- to 2½-pound boneless pork loin roast (single loin)
- ⅓ cup bottled roasted red sweet peppers, drained and chopped
- ¼ cup chopped fresh Italian (flat-leaf) parsley
- ¼ cup pitted green olives, chopped
- 1 tablespoon finely shredded lemon peel
- 2 cloves garlic, minced
- 2 teaspoons snipped fresh thyme or ½ teaspoon dried thyme, crushed
- ¼ teaspoon salt
- ¼ teaspoon coarsely ground black pepper
- 1 recipe Chorizo Custard Dressing *(page 104)* (optional)

PER SERVING: 135 cal., 4 g total fat (1 g sat. fat), 60 mg chol., 183 mg sodium, 1 g carb. (0 g fiber, 0 g sugars), 22 g pro. Exchanges: 3 lean meat.

1 | Preheat oven to 350°F. Trim fat from pork. Using a sharp knife, make a lengthwise cut down the center of the loin, cutting to, but not through, the opposite side. Cut horizontally into the meat, slicing away from the center cut and cutting to, but not through, the opposite side. Repeat on the opposite side. Open so pork is flat. Place plastic wrap over pork. Using the flat side of a meat mallet, pound to an even thickness.

2 | In a small bowl combine roasted sweet peppers, parsley, olives, lemon peel, garlic, and thyme. Spread pepper mixture to an even layer over the roast. Roll the roast into a spiral. Tie roast with 100-percent-cotton kitchen string. Place roast, seam side down, on a rack in a shallow roasting pan. Sprinkle meat with the salt and pepper.

3 | Roast, uncovered, for 50 to 60 minutes or until an instant-read thermometer inserted into center of roast registers 145°F. Remove from oven. Cover meat with foil and let stand for 3 minutes. Remove string before slicing. If desired, serve with Chorizo Custard Dressing.

Ham and Spinach Two-Cheese Pasta

To easily transfer the ramekins in and out of the oven, place them in a shallow baking pan.

SERVINGS 2 (1¼ cups each)
CARB. PER SERVING 37 g
PREP 30 minutes
BAKE 10 minutes

- 2 ounces dried whole grain penne pasta (⅔ cup)
- 1 5-ounce package fresh baby spinach
- 2 teaspoons olive oil
- 1 medium onion, chopped (½ cup)
- 1 tablespoon flour
- ½ teaspoon dry mustard
- ½ teaspoon black pepper
- ½ cup evaporated fat-free milk
- ¼ cup shredded reduced-fat Italian-style cheese blend
- 2 tablespoons shredded Parmesan cheese
- 2 ounces low-sodium ham, cubed

1 Preheat oven to 400°F. In a saucepan cook pasta according to package directions. Place spinach in a large colander in sink. Pour pasta over spinach in colander; drain well. Set aside.

2 In the same saucepan heat oil over medium heat. Add onion; cook about 5 minutes or until tender. Stir in flour, mustard, and pepper. Cook and stir for 1 minute. Add evaporated milk all at once. Cook and stir until slightly thickened. Cook and stir for 1 minute more. Stir in Italian-style cheese and half of the Parmesan cheese. Cook and stir until cheese melts. Stir in pasta mixture and ham; stir gently to coat. Divide mixture between two 10-ounce ramekins or individual casserole dishes. Sprinkle with the remaining Parmesan cheese.

3 Bake, uncovered, about 10 minutes or until tops start to brown.

PER SERVING: 332 cal., 10 g total fat (4 g sat. fat), 27 mg chol., 571 mg sodium, 37 g carb. (5 g fiber, 10 g sugars), 23 g pro. Exchanges: 2 vegetable, 2 starch, 2 lean meat, 1 fat.

Porcini-Rubbed Roast Beef

Porcini mushrooms offer a rich nutty flavor. In North America, these Italian delicacies are most commonly found in dry form.

SERVINGS 8 (4 ounces cooked beef and 2 tablespoons sauce each)
CARB. PER SERVING 5 g
PREP 15 minutes
COOK 15 minutes
ROAST 1 hour 30 minutes
STAND 15 minutes

1 2$\frac{1}{2}$- to 3-pound beef eye of round roast or beef tenderloin roast

2 tablespoons porcini mushroom powder (about 1 ounce)*

1 teaspoon kosher salt

1 teaspoon dried rosemary, finely crushed

$\frac{1}{2}$ teaspoon coarsely ground black pepper

Nonstick cooking spray

1 medium shallot, finely chopped

$\frac{1}{4}$ cup Marsala wine (optional)

1$\frac{1}{2}$ cups lower-sodium beef broth

$\frac{1}{2}$ cup dried porcini mushrooms, coarsely crushed (about 0.5 ounce)

$\frac{1}{4}$ cup fat-free half-and-half

2 teaspoons cornstarch

1 recipe Root Vegetable Puree (page 99) (optional)

1 Preheat oven to 325°F. Trim fat from beef. In a small bowl combine mushroom powder, kosher salt, rosemary, and pepper. Sprinkle the herb mixture evenly over all sides of the meat; rub in with your fingers.

2 Place meat on a rack in a shallow roasting pan. Insert an oven-going meat thermometer into center of roast. If using eye of round roast, roast, uncovered, for 1$\frac{1}{2}$ to 1$\frac{3}{4}$ hours or until thermometer registers 135°F (it is not recommended to roast an eye of round roast past medium rare doneness). If using beef tenderloin roast, increase oven temperature to 425°F. Roast, uncovered, for 35 to 45 minutes or until thermometer registers 135°F (medium rare) or 45 to 50 minutes or until thermometer registers 150°F (medium).

3 Meanwhile, coat a medium skillet with cooking spray; heat skillet over medium heat. Add shallot. Cook for 3 to 5 minutes or until tender, stirring occasionally. If desired, add Marsala wine; cook, uncovered, over medium heat for 3 to 5 minutes or until wine is nearly evaporated. Add beef broth and crushed mushrooms. Bring to boiling; reduce heat. Simmer, uncovered, for 2 minutes. In a small bowl combine half-and-half and cornstarch until smooth. Add to mushroom sauce. Cook and stir until slightly thickened and bubbly; cook and stir for 2 minutes more.

4 Cover meat with foil and let stand for 15 minutes before slicing. Thinly slice meat to serve. Spoon sauce over meat. If desired, serve with Root Vegetable Puree.

*TEST KITCHEN TIP: Find porcini mushroom powder in specialty food markets or order online at *amazon.com*. Or to make your own, place dried porcini mushrooms in a small food processor or spice grinder. Process or grind to a fine powder.

PER SERVING: 186 cal., 4 g total fat (1 g sat. fat), 76 mg chol., 408 mg sodium, 5 g carb. (1 g fiber, 2 g sugars), 31 g pro. Exchanges: 1 vegetable, 4 lean meat.

Coffee-Crusted Beef Tenderloin

If you don't own a meat thermometer, buy one. The internal temperature is important when roasting expensive cuts of meat—if overcooked, the meat is dry.

SERVINGS 10 (4$^{1}/_{2}$ to 5 ounces beef each)
CARB. PER SERVING 3 g or 1 g
PREP 10 minutes
ROAST 50 minutes
STAND 15 minutes

Nonstick cooking spray

2 tablespoons finely ground coffee beans

1 tablespoon packed brown sugar*

1$^{1}/_{2}$ teaspoons garlic powder

1$^{1}/_{2}$ teaspoons paprika

$^{3}/_{4}$ teaspoon kosher salt

$^{3}/_{4}$ teaspoon black pepper

1 4-pound center-cut beef tenderloin roast

Snipped fresh thyme and/or rosemary (optional)

1 Preheat oven to 425°F. Line a 15×10×1-inch baking pan with heavy foil. Place a rack in the pan and coat with cooking spray; set pan aside. For rub, in a small bowl stir together ground coffee, brown sugar, garlic powder, paprika, salt, and pepper; set aside.

2 Trim fat from beef. Place meat on the rack in the prepared baking pan. Sprinkle coffee mixture evenly over top and sides of meat; rub in and press lightly with your fingers.

3 Insert an oven-going meat thermometer into center of meat. Roast, uncovered, for 50 to 60 minutes or until the meat thermometer registers 135°F for medium-rare. Remove from oven.

4 Cover meat with foil; let stand for 15 minutes before slicing. (Temperature of the meat after standing should be 145°F.) Cut meat into $^{1}/_{2}$-inch-thick slices. If desired, garnish with thyme and/or rosemary.

MAKE-AHEAD DIRECTIONS: Prepare as directed through Step 2. Cover and chill for up to 24 hours. Continue as directed in Step 3.

*SUGAR SUBSTITUTE: Choose Sugar Twin Brown. Follow package directions to use product amount equivalent to 1 tablespoon brown sugar.

PER SERVING: 233 cal., 10 g total fat (4 g sat. fat), 94 mg chol., 230 mg sodium, 3 g carb. (0 g fiber, 1 g sugars), 32 g pro. Exchanges: 4.5 lean meat, 0.5 fat.

PER SERVING WITH SUBSTITUTE: Same as above, except 229 cal., 1 g carb. (0 g sugars).

QUICK TIP
Be sure to cover the roasted beef and let it stand for 15 minutes before slicing. This standing time helps lock in the juices.

Slow-Roasted Beef with Soy-Apricot Sauce

Perfect for holiday entertaining, this one-pot meal allows you to mingle with your guests instead of spending time in the kitchen.

SERVINGS 8 (about 3 ounces cooked beef, $^{3}/_{4}$ cup vegetables, and about $1^{1}/_{2}$ tablespoons sauce each)
CARB. PER SERVING 17 g
PREP 30 minutes
BAKE 2 hours

- 1 2$^{1}/_{2}$- to 3-pound boneless beef arm pot roast
- 1 teaspoon fennel seeds, crushed
- 1 teaspoon ground coriander
- $^{1}/_{2}$ teaspoon salt
- $^{1}/_{2}$ teaspoon crushed red pepper
- $^{1}/_{4}$ teaspoon ground cardamom
- $^{1}/_{4}$ teaspoon ground ginger
- 1 tablespoon canola oil
- 2 large fennel bulbs, trimmed, cored, and cut into 1$^{1}/_{2}$-inch-thick wedges
- 2 medium shallots, peeled and quartered
- $^{3}/_{4}$ cup apricot nectar
- $^{1}/_{4}$ cup reduced-sodium soy sauce
- $^{1}/_{2}$ head napa cabbage, cored and cut crosswise into 2-inch-wide slices
- 2 medium red sweet peppers, seeded and cut into 1-inch-thick slices
- 2 cups fresh sugar snap pea pods, trimmed
- 2 tablespoons lemon juice
- 2 tablespoons sesame seeds, toasted

1 Preheat oven to 325°F. Trim fat from beef. In a small bowl combine fennel seeds, coriander, salt, crushed red pepper, cardamom, and ginger. Sprinkle evenly over meat, rubbing in with your fingers. In a 5$^{1}/_{2}$- or 6-quart oven-going Dutch oven heat oil over medium heat. Add meat; cook until browned, turning to brown all sides evenly. Remove meat from pan and set aside.

2 Arrange fennel wedges and shallots in an even layer in the Dutch oven. Add apricot nectar and soy sauce to the pan. Place meat on top of vegetables. Bring liquid in pan to boiling. Cover pan and transfer to the oven. Bake for 1$^{1}/_{2}$ hours.

3 Uncover and spoon pan juices over meat. Arrange cabbage, sweet peppers, and pea pods around the roast. Cover and bake about 30 minutes more or until meat and vegetables are tender.

4 Transfer vegetables and meat to a large platter; cover to keep warm. Bring pan juices to boiling over high heat. Boil about 8 minutes or until reduced to $^{3}/_{4}$ cup. Remove pan from heat. Stir in lemon juice. To serve, spoon juices over meat and vegetables and sprinkle with sesame seeds.

PER SERVING: 286 cal., 10 g total fat (3 g sat. fat), 94 mg chol., 572 mg sodium, 17 g carb. (5 g fiber, 7 g sugars), 34 g pro. Exchanges: 2 vegetable, 0.5 starch, 4 lean meat, 0.5 fat.

Beef and Vegetable Biscuit Bake

Half the package of biscuits is used for this recipe, so bake those remaining as directed on the package. Serve them for breakfast.

SERVINGS 5 (1 cup meat mixture and 1 biscuit each)
CARB. PER SERVING 34 g
PREP 25 minutes
ROAST 20 minutes
BAKE 12 minutes

Nonstick cooking spray

12 ounces fresh Brussels sprouts, halved

5 medium carrots, sliced (2$\frac{1}{2}$ cups)

2 teaspoons olive oil

1 teaspoon dried thyme, crushed

$\frac{1}{4}$ teaspoon black pepper

8 ounces extra-lean ground beef

1 medium onion, chopped ($\frac{1}{2}$ cup)

5 teaspoons butter

3 tablespoons flour

$\frac{1}{4}$ teaspoon salt

1 cup fat-free milk

$\frac{3}{4}$ cup water

4 ounces fresh mushrooms, chopped

$\frac{1}{2}$ of a 12-ounce package refrigerated biscuits (5), such as Pillsbury Grands! Jr. brand

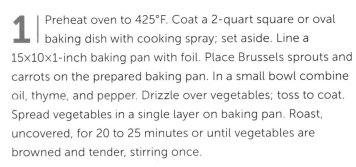

1 | Preheat oven to 425°F. Coat a 2-quart square or oval baking dish with cooking spray; set aside. Line a 15×10×1-inch baking pan with foil. Place Brussels sprouts and carrots on the prepared baking pan. In a small bowl combine oil, thyme, and pepper. Drizzle over vegetables; toss to coat. Spread vegetables in a single layer on baking pan. Roast, uncovered, for 20 to 25 minutes or until vegetables are browned and tender, stirring once.

2 | Meanwhile, in a large skillet cook meat and onion over medium heat until meat is browned and onion is tender, using a wooden spoon to break up meat as it cooks. Remove from skillet; drain. Set aside.

3 | In the same large skillet melt butter over medium heat. In a bowl combine flour and salt; carefully add about half of the flour mixture to the milk, whisking until smooth. Add the remaining flour mixture to the melted butter, whisking until well mixed. Add the flour-milk mixture and the water all at once to the butter mixture in skillet. Cook and stir until thickened and bubbly; cook and stir for 2 minutes more. Stir in mushrooms, roasted vegetables, and cooked meat mixture; heat through.

4 | Spoon meat-vegetable mixture into the prepared baking dish. Top with the biscuits. Bake for 12 to 15 minutes or until biscuits are golden brown and casserole is bubbly.

PER SERVING: 309 cal., 12 g total fat (5 g sat. fat), 39 mg chol., 621 mg sodium, 34 g carb. (5 g fiber, 10 g sugars), 17 g pro. Exchanges: 2 vegetable, 1.5 starch, 2 lean meat, 1 fat.

BBQ Spice-Rubbed Turkey Breast

If you plan to carve the turkey at the table, lightly brush a little of the sauce over the breast halves for a glistening presentation.

SERVINGS 10 (5½ to 6 ounces cooked turkey and 3 tablespoons sauce each)
CARB. PER SERVING 23 g or 20 g
PREP 30 minutes
ROAST 1 hour 20 minutes
STAND 10 minutes

2 3- to 3½-pound fresh or frozen bone-in turkey breast halves

Nonstick cooking spray

2 tablespoons packed dark brown sugar*

2 teaspoons garlic powder

2 teaspoons paprika

1 teaspoon ground cumin

1 teaspoon chili powder

¾ teaspoon black pepper

½ teaspoon salt

1 recipe Cranberry Barbecue Sauce

PER SERVING: 392 cal., 14 g total fat (3 g sat. fat), 123 mg chol., 550 mg sodium, 23 g carb. (1 g fiber, 15 g sugars), 41 g pro. Exchanges: 1.5 carb., 5.5 lean meat, 1 fat.

PER SERVING WITH SUBSTITUTE: Same as above, except 381 cal., 20 g carb. (13 g sugars). Exchanges: 1 carb.

1 Thaw turkey, if frozen. Preheat oven to 400°F. Coat a large shallow roasting pan and rack with cooking spray. In a small bowl combine brown sugar, garlic powder, paprika, cumin, chili powder, pepper, and salt. Set aside.

2 Place turkey breast halves on parchment paper or waxed paper. Starting at breast bone of each turkey half, slip fingers between the skin and meat to loosen skin, leaving skin partially attached at edges. Lift skin and spread spice mixture evenly under skin over breast meat. Insert an oven-going meat thermometer into thickest part of breast halves without touching bone. Place turkey breast halves, bone sides down, on roasting rack in the prepared pan.**

3 Roast on lower rack of oven for 20 minutes. Reduce oven temperature to 350°F. Roast for 1 to 1½ hours more or until thermometer registers 165°F, occasionally spooning pan juices over turkey.

4 Remove turkey from oven. Cover with foil; let stand for 10 minutes before slicing. Serve with Cranberry Barbecue Sauce.

CRANBERRY BARBECUE SAUCE: In a medium saucepan cook 1 cup chopped onion in 1 tablespoon hot vegetable oil over medium heat for about 5 minutes or until tender. Stir in one 14-ounce can whole cranberry sauce, ⅓ cup bottled chili sauce, 1 tablespoon cider vinegar, 1 tablespoon Worcestershire sauce, and ¼ teaspoon freshly ground black pepper. Bring to boiling; reduce heat. Simmer, uncovered, for about 5 minutes or until thickened, stirring occasionally. Pass with BBQ Spice-Rubbed Turkey Breast.

***SUGAR SUBSTITUTES:** Choose from Sweet'N Low Brown or Sugar Twin Granulated Brown. Follow package directions to use product amount equivalent to 2 tablespoons brown sugar.

****TEST KITCHEN TIP:** To simplify the preparation, you can rub the spice mixture onto the outside of each turkey breast for a crusty appearance. To prevent burning, cover turkey breasts with foil for the last 30 minutes of roasting.

Turkey-Mushroom Pasta with Maple-Cream Sauce

If you have leftover holiday turkey, shred some to use in this delicious carbonara-style pasta dish.

SERVINGS 6 (1 cup each)
CARB. PER SERVING 41 g
PREP 35 minutes
COOK 25 minutes

- 2 cups fresh cremini or button mushrooms, thinly sliced
- 2 medium leeks, trimmed and thinly sliced ($^3/_4$ cup)
- 2 cloves garlic, minced
- 1 tablespoon olive oil
- 6 ounces dried whole grain linguine or dried multigrain spaghetti
- 2 medium parsnips, peeled and cut into long julienne strips (2 cups)
- $^3/_4$ cup fat-free half-and-half
- $^1/_4$ cup reduced-calorie maple-flavor syrup
- $^1/_2$ teaspoon salt
- 2 cups coarsely shredded cooked turkey
- 2 tablespoons snipped fresh sage or $1^1/_2$ teaspoons dried sage, crushed
- $^1/_2$ cup refrigerated or frozen egg product, thawed
- 3 slices turkey bacon, cooked according to package directions and crumbled
- Freshly ground black pepper

1 | In a very large nonstick skillet cook mushrooms, leeks, and garlic in hot oil over medium heat about 6 minutes or until mushrooms are tender and leeks are starting to brown, stirring occasionally.

2 | Meanwhile, cook linguine according to package directions, adding parsnips for the last 4 minutes of cooking time. Drain and keep warm.

3 | Add half-and-half, syrup, and salt to the mushroom mixture. Cook and stir just until boiling. Add turkey, sage, and drained pasta mixture. Cook and toss for 2 to 3 minutes to heat through. Remove from the heat. Add egg and quickly toss to coat (mixture may appear curdled).

4 | Divide pasta mixture among six shallow bowls. Top with bacon and sprinkle with pepper.

PER SERVING: 320 cal., 7 g total fat (2 g sat. fat), 54 mg chol., 480 mg sodium, 41 g carb. (6 g fiber, 11 g sugars), 24 g pro. Exchanges: 2 vegetable, 1.5 starch, 0.5 carb., 2.5 lean meat, 0.5 fat.

Chicken Pot Pies

For a decorative edge, cut the pastry circle with a fluted pastry wheel or a scalloped-edge round cookie cutter.

SERVINGS 2 (1 pot pie each)
CARB. PER SERVING 35 g
PREP 50 minutes
BAKE 20 minutes
COOL 10 minutes

- 1/2 cup whole wheat flour
- 1 tablespoon refrigerated or frozen egg product, thawed
- 2 teaspoons tub-style vegetable oil spread
- 1/4 teaspoon baking powder
- Ice water
- 1 tablespoon olive oil
- 1 medium carrot, chopped (1/2 cup)
- 1 stalk celery, chopped (1/2 cup)
- 1 small onion, chopped (1/3 cup)
- 1/3 cup chopped fresh mushrooms
- 2 cloves garlic, minced
- 3/4 cup reduced-sodium chicken broth
- 1/4 teaspoon dried thyme, crushed
- 1/4 teaspoon black pepper
- 1/8 teaspoon salt
- 3/4 cup chopped cooked chicken breast
- 1/4 cup plain fat-free Greek yogurt
- 1/4 cup frozen peas
- 2 tablespoons snipped fresh parsley
- 1 egg white, lightly beaten

PER SERVING: 364 cal., 13 g total fat (2 g sat. fat), 45 mg chol., 584 mg sodium, 35 g carb. (7 g fiber, 6 g sugars), 29 g pro. Exchanges: 1.5 vegetable, 2 starch, 3 lean meat, 1 fat.

1 For the dough, set aside 1 tablespoon of the whole wheat flour. In a food processor combine remaining whole wheat flour, the egg, vegetable oil spread, and baking powder. Cover and process just until combined. Add enough ice water, 1 teaspoon at a time, to make mixture that forms a loose dough and holds together when pinched. Remove dough from processor; knead dough a few times by hand and form into a ball. Wrap in plastic wrap and refrigerate while preparing filling.

2 For the filling, in a large skillet heat oil over medium heat. Add carrot, celery, onion, mushrooms, and garlic; cook about 5 minutes or just until softened. Sprinkle the reserved 1 tablespoon flour over vegetables; cook and stir for 1 minute more. Add chicken broth all at once. Cook and stir until slightly thickened and bubbly.

3 In a small bowl stir together thyme, pepper, and salt; set aside a pinch of the thyme mixture. Add the remaining thyme mixture to the vegetable mixture. Stir in chicken, yogurt, peas, and parsley until combined. Divide chicken mixture evenly between two 8-ounce ramekins, individual casseroles, or 10-ounce custard cups.

4 Preheat oven to 400°F. Line a baking sheet with foil; set aside. Remove dough from refrigerator. Divide dough in half. Roll out each dough half into a circle slightly larger than the circumference of a ramekin (cut dough to fit if necessary). Place dough circles on top of the filling in the ramekins, pressing down slightly along each edge to secure. Make a 1/2-inch opening or a few small slits in the crust to allow steam to escape.

5 Brush the egg white over crusts; sprinkle with reserved seasoning mixture. Place ramekins on prepared baking sheet. Bake for 20 to 25 minutes or until crust is lightly browned. Allow pies to cool 10 minutes before serving.

Fennel-Orange Chicken with Roasted Beets and Grapes

Remove and discard the golden skin as you carve the succulent meat.

SERVINGS 8 (3 ounces cooked chicken,
1 cluster grapes, ³/₄ cup arugula, and scant 1 cup beets each)
CARB. PER SERVING 28 g
PREP 30 minutes
ROAST 1 hour 30 minutes
STAND 15 minutes

2 teaspoons finely shredded orange peel

1¹/₂ teaspoons fennel seeds, crushed

1 teaspoon coarsely ground black pepper

¹/₂ teaspoon salt

1 5- to 6-pound whole roasting chicken

8 medium beets (about 3 pounds), trimmed, peeled, and cut into ³/₄-inch-thick wedges

1 tablespoon olive oil

2 teaspoons snipped fresh thyme or ¹/₂ teaspoon dried thyme, crushed

¹/₄ teaspoon salt

¹/₄ teaspoon coarsely ground black pepper

1 pound seedless red grapes on the stem, cut into 8 small clusters

6 cups fresh arugula

3 tablespoons orange juice

4 ounces semisoft goat cheese (chèvre) or reduced-fat feta cheese, crumbled

PER SERVING: 348 cal., 11 g total fat (4 g sat. fat), 106 mg chol., 513 mg sodium, 28 g carb. (6 g fiber, 21 g sugars), 36 g pro. Exchanges: 2 vegetable, 1 fruit, 4.5 lean meat, 1 fat.

1 Preheat oven to 375°F. In a small bowl combine orange peel, fennel seeds, 1 teaspoon pepper, and ¹/₂ teaspoon salt. Remove giblets and neck from chicken if present and discard or save for another use. Gently slide your fingers under the skin of the chicken that is over the breast and thighs without tearing the skin. Spoon orange peel mixture under skin and use your fingers to spread it evenly over breast and thigh meat.

2 Fold chicken neck skin onto chicken back; secure with a small skewer. Tie drumsticks to tail with 100-percent-cotton kitchen string. Tie wings close to body or twist wing tips under back of the chicken. Place chicken, breast side up, on a rack in a shallow roasting pan. If desired, insert an oven-going meat thermometer into center of inside thigh muscle. (Thermometer should not touch bone.) Roast, uncovered, for 40 minutes.

3 Meanwhile, in a large bowl combine beets, oil, thyme, ¹/₄ teaspoon salt, and ¹/₄ teaspoon pepper. Arrange beets in an even layer around chicken in roasting pan. Cut band of skin or string between drumsticks. Roast for 40 minutes more, stirring beets after 20 minutes. Add the grape clusters and roast for 10 minutes more or until drumsticks move easily in their sockets and chicken is no longer pink (180°F in thigh*). Remove from oven and cover chicken with foil. Let stand for 15 minutes before carving.

4 Transfer chicken to a serving platter. Arrange beets, grape clusters, and *fresh thyme sprigs* around chicken. In a large bowl toss together arugula and orange juice. Divide arugula among eight serving plates. Pass platter with chicken, beets, and grapes and a bowl of goat cheese.

*TEST KITCHEN TIP: If thermometer in chicken registers 180°F before the beets are done, transfer chicken to a platter. Cover and start standing time while the beets finish roasting.

QUICK TIP
Serve this beautifully roasted chicken like a salad. Simply divide the arugula, beets, and grapes among the plates. Top with carved chicken and sprinkle with feta cheese.

Chicken-Noodle Casserole

If you opt to use whole grain bread instead white bread for making the crumb topping, expect the top to be more brown than golden.

SERVINGS 8 (1¼ cups each)
CARB. PER SERVING 33 g
PREP 15 minutes
COOK 35 minutes
BAKE 30 minutes

4 stalks celery, chopped (2 cups)

1 medium onion, chopped (½ cup)

2 teaspoons canola oil

2 pounds chicken legs and/or thighs, skinned

½ teaspoon black pepper

1 teaspoon dried thyme, crushed

¾ teaspoon salt

6 cups water

1 slice bread

10 ounces jumbo or extra-large egg noodles

1 8-ounce carton light sour cream

2 tablespoons flour

½ teaspoon garlic powder

Nonstick cooking spray

2 tablespoons snipped fresh parsley

PER SERVING: 288 cal., 9 g total fat (3 g sat. fat), 98 mg chol., 340 mg sodium, 33 g carb. (2 g fiber, 2 g sugars), 19 g pro. Exchanges: 2 starch, 2 lean meat, 1 fat.

1 Preheat oven to 375°F. In a Dutch oven cook two-thirds of the celery and onion in hot oil over medium heat for 3 minutes. Add chicken, pepper, thyme, and salt to Dutch oven; cook for 2 minutes. Add the water. Bring to boiling; reduce heat. Simmer, covered, for 20 to 25 minutes until chicken is no longer pink.

2 Meanwhile, for topping, tear bread into small pieces. Finely chop remaining celery and onion. In a small bowl toss together the bread, celery, and onion; set aside.

3 Using a slotted spoon, transfer chicken to a cutting board to cool slightly. Add noodles to simmering broth in Dutch oven; boil gently for 7 to 8 minutes, just until tender, stirring occasionally. With a slotted spoon, transfer noodles, celery, and onion to a 3-quart baking dish.

4 For sauce, in a bowl whisk together sour cream, flour, and garlic powder. Gradually whisk in 1 cup of the hot broth until smooth. Add sour cream mixture to broth in Dutch oven; cook and stir until boiling.

5 Meanwhile, remove chicken from bones; discard bones. Chop chicken and add to noodles in baking dish. Gently stir in sauce. Sprinkle with bread topping, then lightly coat with cooking spray.

6 Bake, uncovered, for 30 to 35 minutes or until casserole is heated through and topping begins to brown. Top with parsley just before serving.

Mixed Satay Skewers

Perfect for serving a crowd—the beef, chicken, and tofu options offer something for everyone.

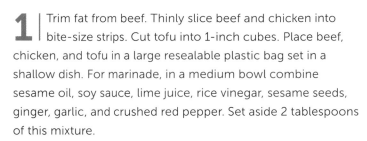

SERVINGS 12 (1 skewer and 1 tablespoon yogurt sauce each)
CARB. PER SERVING 2 g or 5 g
PREP 30 minutes
MARINATE 1 hour
GRILL 6 minutes

- 12 ounces beef flank steak
- 12 ounces skinless, boneless chicken breast
- 1 12-ounce package extra-firm water-packed tofu, patted dry
- 2 tablespoons toasted sesame oil
- 2 tablespoons low-sodium soy sauce
- 4 teaspoons lime juice
- 4 teaspoons rice vinegar
- 1 tablespoon toasted sesame seeds
- 2 teaspoons minced fresh ginger
- 4 cloves garlic, minced
- 1/2 teaspoon crushed red pepper
- 12 10-inch wooden or metal skewers
- 1/2 cup plain fat-free yogurt
- 3 tablespoons peanut butter
- Snipped fresh cilantro (optional)

1 Trim fat from beef. Thinly slice beef and chicken into bite-size strips. Cut tofu into 1-inch cubes. Place beef, chicken, and tofu in a large resealable plastic bag set in a shallow dish. For marinade, in a medium bowl combine sesame oil, soy sauce, lime juice, rice vinegar, sesame seeds, ginger, garlic, and crushed red pepper. Set aside 2 tablespoons of this mixture.

2 Pour remaining marinade over meat and tofu; seal bag. Turn to coat. Marinate in the refrigerator for 1 hour. If using wooden skewers, soak them in water for 30 minutes before using.

3 Drain beef, chicken, and tofu, discarding marinade. On four wooden or metal skewers thread beef accordion-style. On another four skewers thread chicken accordion style. Skewer cubes of tofu on remaining four skewers, leaving a 1/4-inch space between pieces.

4 Place filled skewers on a greased grill rack directly over medium coals. Grill, uncovered, for 6 to 8 minutes or until beef is slightly pink in the center and chicken is no longer pink, turning once halfway through grilling. (Or broil on the unheated rack of a broiler pan 4 to 5 inches from heat about 6 to 8 minutes, turning once halfway through broiling.)

5 Meanwhile, in a small bowl combine yogurt and peanut butter. Add the 2 tablespoons reserved marinade mixture. Stir to combine.

6 Serve satay skewers with yogurt dipping sauce. If desired, garnish with cilantro.

PER BEEF SKEWER: 177 cal., 9 g total fat (3 g sat. fat), 53 mg chol., 169 mg sodium, 2 g carb (0 g fiber, 1 g sugars), 20 g pro. Exchanges: 3 lean meat, 1 fat.

PER CHICKEN SKEWER: 153 cal., 7 g total fat (1 g sat. fat), 54 mg chol., 201 mg sodium, 2 g carb (0 g fiber, 1 g sugars), 20 g pro. Exchanges: 3 lean meat.

PER TOFU SKEWER: 143 cal., 9 g total fat (1 g sat. fat), 0 mg chol., 122 mg sodium, 5 g carb (1 g fiber, 1 g sugars), 11 g pro. Exchanges: 1.5 lean meat, 1 vegetable, 1 fat.

Crusted Grouper with Mint-Artichoke Salad

Fresh-made soft bread crumbs combined with olive oil transform into a crispy golden crust when baked in a hot oven .

SERVINGS 4 (1 fish fillet and about ²/₃ cup salad each)
CARB. PER SERVING 15 g
PREP 20 minutes
BAKE 4 minutes

4 4- to 6-ounce fresh or frozen skinless grouper or cod fillets

½ teaspoon paprika

¼ teaspoon salt

¼ teaspoon black pepper

2 slices whole grain bread

2 tablespoons olive oil

2 6- to 6.5-ounce jars marinated artichoke hearts

1 medium red sweet pepper, cut into thin bite-size strips

¼ cup pitted Kalamata olives, coarsely chopped

1 tablespoon snipped fresh mint

1 teaspoon snipped fresh rosemary

1 clove garlic, minced

1 Thaw fish, if frozen. Preheat oven to 425°F. Rinse fish; pat dry with paper towels. Place fish on a lightly greased baking sheet. Measure thickness of fish. In a small bowl combine paprika, salt, and black pepper; sprinkle evenly over fish.

2 Tear bread into large pieces and place in a food processor; cover and pulse with several on-off turns to make very large crumbs. You should have about 1½ cups. Transfer bread to a small bowl and add oil; toss to coat. Spoon bread crumbs evenly over fish fillets.

3 Bake fish for 4 to 6 minutes per ½-inch thickness or until fish flakes easily when tested with a fork, tenting with foil toward the end of baking time if needed to avoid overbrowning.

4 Meanwhile, for artichoke salad, drain artichoke hearts, reserving 1 tablespoon of the marinade. Coarsely chop artichoke hearts. In a small bowl combine artichoke hearts, reserved marinade, sweet pepper, olives, mint, rosemary, and garlic.

5 To serve, place 1 fish fillet on each of four serving plates. Divide artichoke salad evenly over fish.

15
grams
carb

PER SERVING: 280 cal., 14 g total fat (1 g sat. fat), 42 mg chol., 582 mg sodium, 15 g carb. (2 g fiber, 2 g sugars), 25 g pro. Exchanges: 2 vegetable, 0.5 starch, 3 lean meat, 2 fat.

Lobster Tails with Lemon-Chamomile Sesame Sauce

The lemony tea-infused dipping sauce is a light and tasty replacement for traditional clarified butter.

SERVINGS 4 (4 ounces cooked lobster and about 2 tablespoons sauce each)
CARB. PER SERVING 3 g
PREP 20 minutes
COOK 6 minutes
BAKE 10 minutes

4   8- to 10-ounce fresh or frozen lobster tails

⅛   teaspoon salt

⅛   teaspoon ground ginger

⅛   teaspoon cayenne pepper

1   chamomile tea bag

⅓   cup boiling water

3   tablespoons lemon juice

3   tablespoons untoasted sesame oil

⅛   teaspoon salt

PER SERVING: 218 cal., 11 g total fat (2 g sat. fat), 92 mg chol., 630 mg sodium, 3 g carb. (0 g fiber, 0 g sugars), 26 g pro. Exchanges: 4 lean meat, 1.5 fat.

1 | Preheat oven to 425°F. Thaw lobster, if frozen. Rinse lobster; pat dry with paper towels. Butterfly tails by using kitchen shears or a sharp knife to cut lengthwise through centers of hard top shells and meat, cutting to, but not through, bottoms of shells. Press shell halves of tails apart with your fingers.

2 | Grease an indoor grill pan; heat pan over medium-high heat. Add two of the lobster tails, meat sides down, to the hot pan. Cook for 3 to 4 minutes or until browned. Transfer lobster tails to a 15×10×1-inch baking pan, placing them meat sides up. Repeat with remaining 2 lobster tails.

3 | In a small bowl combine ⅛ teaspoon salt, the ginger, and cayenne pepper. Sprinkle evenly over lobster tails. Bake for 10 to 12 minutes or until lobster meat is opaque.

4 | Meanwhile, for sauce, place tea bag in a small mug; add the boiling water and steep for 3 minutes. Remove tea bag, squeezing bag. In a small bowl whisk together tea, lemon juice, sesame oil, and remaining ⅛ teaspoon salt. To serve, place a lobster tail on each of four serving plates. Drizzle each tail with about 1 tablespoon of the sauce. Serve remaining sauce in little cups to use for dipping.

QUICK TIP

If an indoor grill pan is not a member of your pan collection, use a large stove-top griddle or skillet.

Quinoa Salmon Cups

Protein-rich quinoa combines with salmon to create these baked cups that are a healthful new take on the old-fashioned salmon patties.

SERVINGS 6 (2 salmon cups, 1 cup arugula, and 2 tablespoons sauce each)
CARB. PER SERVING 26 g
PREP 20 minutes
BAKE 25 minutes
COOL 10 minutes

- 2   cups cooked quinoa
- 2   6-ounce pouches pink chunk salmon, drained
- 1   medium onion, finely chopped (½ cup)
- 2   tablespoons snipped fresh chives
- 2   cloves garlic, minced
- 1   cup panko (Japanese-style bread crumbs)
- ¾   teaspoon lemon-pepper seasoning
- ½   cup fat-free milk
- 2   eggs, lightly beaten
- 2   egg whites, lightly beaten
- 2   tablespoons olive oil
- Nonstick cooking spray
- 1   6-ounce carton plain fat-free Greek yogurt
- 1   tablespoon Dijon-style mustard
- 1   tablespoon snipped fresh chives
- 2   teaspoons lemon juice
- Freshly ground black pepper
- 6   cups arugula
- 1   lemon, cut into thin wedges
- Snipped fresh chives (optional)

PER SERVING: 279 cal., 10 g total fat (2 g sat. fat), 82 mg chol., 485 mg sodium, 26 g carb. (3 g fiber, 4 g sugars), 22 g pro. Exchanges: 1.5 starch, 2.5 medium-fat meat.

1 Preheat oven to 350°F. In a large bowl stir together cooked quinoa, the salmon, onion, the 2 tablespoons chives, and the garlic.

2 In a bowl stir together panko and lemon-pepper seasoning; add milk, eggs, egg whites, and oil, stirring until combined. Add panko mixture to salmon mixture; stir until well mixed.

3 Generously coat twelve 2½-inch muffin cups with cooking spray. Divide salmon-panko mixture evenly among the prepared cups, using a heaping ⅓ cup in each.

4 Bake about 25 minutes or until tops are golden and an instant-read thermometer inserted in center of a cup registers 160°F. Cool in muffin cups on a wire rack for 10 minutes.

5 Meanwhile, for lemon-mustard sauce, stir together yogurt, mustard, the 1 tablespoon chives, the lemon juice, and black pepper. Divide arugula among six serving plates. Run a knife around the edges of each cup to loosen; remove from muffin cups. Arrange warm salmon cups on top of arugula. Serve with lemon-mustard sauce and lemon wedges. If desired, sprinkle with additional snipped chives.

Spiced Acorn Squash with Pan-Roasted Cauliflower and Greens

Traditional acorn squash has dark green skin. A newer golden variety is becoming popular. Use either color for this meatless main dish.

SERVINGS 4 (1 squash half, 1¼ cups cauliflower mixture, about ½ cup chard, ½ ounce cheese, and ½ tablespoon pine nuts each)
CARB. PER SERVING 32 g
PREP 35 minutes
BAKE 40 minutes
COOK 13 minutes

2 1- to 1¼-pound acorn squash
½ teaspoon ground coriander
¼ teaspoon salt
¼ teaspoon crushed red pepper
¼ teaspoon ground allspice
¼ teaspoon ground cumin
1½ tablespoons canola oil
6 cups cauliflower florets
1 small onion, cut into thin wedges
¼ teaspoon black pepper
⅛ teaspoon salt
8 cups coarsely torn Swiss chard
1 clove garlic, minced
⅓ cup reduced-fat unsweetened coconut milk
2 ounces reduced-fat feta cheese, crumbled
2 tablespoons pine nuts, toasted, or roasted unsalted pistachio nuts

1 Preheat oven to 350°F. Line a shallow baking pan with parchment paper or foil. Cut each squash in half. Scoop out seeds and discard. Place squash halves, cut sides down, in prepared pan. Bake for 30 minutes.

2 In a small bowl combine coriander, salt, crushed red pepper, allspice, and cumin. Turn squash flesh sides up. Sprinkle evenly with spice mixture. Bake, uncovered, for 10 to 15 minutes more or until squash is tender.

3 Meanwhile, add oil to a very large nonstick skillet; preheat over medium heat. Add cauliflower and onion; sprinkle with black pepper and ⅛ teaspoon salt. Cook cauliflower, covered, over medium heat for 5 minutes, stirring once. Uncover and cook for 5 to 8 minutes more or until cauliflower is just tender, stirring occasionally. Remove cauliflower from the pan and keep warm.

4 Add chard and garlic to the same pan. Cook about 2 minutes or until chard is tender, tossing occasionally with tongs. Remove from heat. Add coconut milk. To serve, place one squash half, flesh side up, on each of four serving plates. Spoon chard mixture evenly into squash bowls and top with cauliflower mixture allowing vegetables to spill out of squash. Sprinkle evenly with feta cheese and nuts.

PER SERVING: 246 cal., 12 g total fat (3 g sat. fat), 4 mg chol., 623 mg sodium, 32 g carb. (8 g fiber, 5 g sugars), 10 g pro. Exchanges: 2 vegetable, 1 starch, 0.5 lean meat, 2 fat.

5

seasonal
sides and salads

It's often a succulent roast or golden bird that is the center of the

holiday table, but it's the bowls of flavorful sides that round out

the meal and tantalize the taste buds. From beans to Brussels

sprouts and fruit salads to slaws, these dishes are celebration-

worthy and good for you, too.

Sweet Curry Carrots with Chive Yogurt

Warm honey combines with curry powder to create a sweet glaze. After drizzling the carrots with the honey mixture, toss and turn them to evenly coat.

SERVINGS 6 (³⁄4 cup and 2 tablespoons sauce each)
CARB. PER SERVING 20 g
PREP 20 minutes
ROAST 25 minutes

1½ pounds carrots with tops, trimmed (about 10)

1 tablespoon extra virgin olive oil

3 tablespoons honey

1 tablespoon curry powder

²⁄3 cup plain low-fat Greek yogurt

¼ cup snipped fresh chives

¼ teaspoon salt

PER SERVING: 116 cal., 3 g total fat (1 g sat. fat), 1 mg chol., 177 mg sodium, 20 g carb. (3 g fiber, 15 g sugars), 4 g pro. Exchanges: 2 vegetable, 0.5 carb., 0.5 fat.

1 Preheat oven to 425°F. Scrub carrots; peel if desired. Halve any large carrots lengthwise.

2 Line a 15×10×1-inch baking pan with foil. Toss carrots with olive oil. Evenly spread carrots in prepared pan. Roast carrots for 15 minutes. Meanwhile, in a small microwave-safe bowl warm honey in microwave on 100 percent power (high) for 15 to 30 seconds. Whisk in curry powder; set aside.

3 Remove carrots from oven. Drizzle with honey mixture; toss to coat. Roast about 10 minutes longer, turning occasionally, until carrots are glazed and tender when pierced with a fork. Transfer to a serving bowl.

4 For chive yogurt, in a bowl combine yogurt, chives, and salt. Serve with roasted carrots.

Haricots Verts with Herb Butter

Once steamed, immediately transfer the beans to the platter or plates and start topping them with small spoonfuls of butter so it will melt.

SERVINGS 4 (1 cup beans and about 1 tablespoon butter each)
CARB. PER SERVING 7 g
PREP 15 minutes
COOK 5 minutes

- 2 tablespoons butter, softened
- 1 tablespoon very finely chopped onion
- 2 teaspoons snipped fresh tarragon
- 1 clove garlic, minced
- ½ teaspoon finely shredded lemon peel
- ¼ teaspoon salt
- ¼ teaspoon black pepper
- 12 ounces haricots verts or other small, thin green beans (4 cups)

1 In a small bowl by hand beat together butter, onion, tarragon, garlic, lemon peel, salt, and pepper. Cover and chill until ready to use.

2 Rinse beans. If desired, trim tips off beans; drain. Place a steamer basket in a large skillet. Add water to just below the bottom of basket. Bring to boiling. Add beans. Cover and steam for 5 to 6 minutes or until crisp-tender; drain.

3 To serve, place green beans on a serving platter or on four serving plates. Top with small spoonfuls of the herbed butter. Spread butter over beans.

PER SERVING: 80 cal., 6 g total fat (4 g sat. fat), 15 mg chol., 202 mg sodium, 7 g carb. (2 g fiber, 3 g sugars), 2 g pro. Exchanges: 1 vegetable, 1 fat.

7 grams carb

Butternut Squash and Quinoa Pilaf

Follow the package directions to prepare the quinoa. It takes about 20 minutes to cook while the squash is roasting.

SERVINGS 8 (¹/₂ cup each)
CARB. PER SERVING 19 g
PREP 25 minutes
ROAST 30 minutes

4 cups peeled and cubed butternut squash

6 cloves garlic, minced

¹/₈ to ¹/₄ teaspoon crushed red pepper

5 teaspoons olive oil

¹/₄ cup sliced almonds

2 cups cooked quinoa

1 tablespoon snipped fresh sage

¹/₂ teaspoon salt

Fresh sage leaves (optional)

1 Preheat oven to 425°F. In a large bowl combine butternut squash, garlic, and crushed red pepper. Drizzle with 2 teaspoons of the oil. Stir until the squash is evenly coated. Spoon into a 15x10x1-inch baking pan. Roast for 30 minutes, stirring once and adding the sliced almonds for the last 4 to 5 minutes of roasting.

2 In a large bowl combine quinoa, the remaining 3 teaspoons oil, the snipped sage, and salt. Stir in roasted squash and almonds. If desired, garnish with sage leaves.

4 grams protein

PER SERVING: 132 cal., 5 g total fat (1 g sat. fat), 0 mg chol., 152 mg sodium, 19 g carb. (3 g fiber, 2 g sugars), 4 g pro. Exchanges: 1 starch, 1 fat.

QUICK TIP
For a flavor change, you can substitute chopped walnuts or pecans for the sliced almonds and fresh basil or parsley for the fresh sage.

Tomato and Pepper Sweet Potatoes

Unlike fresh tomatoes, canned tomatoes are an excellent source of the antioxidant lycopene, which may help lower the risk of heart disease.

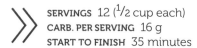

SERVINGS 12 (¹/₂ cup each)
CARB. PER SERVING 16 g
START TO FINISH 35 minutes

4 cups bite-size sweet potato chunks (about 1¹/₂ pounds)

1 tablespoon olive oil

2 medium onions, thinly sliced

2 medium green sweet peppers, thinly sliced

2 14.5-ounce cans Italian-style stewed tomatoes, undrained and cut up

¹/₂ teaspoon packed brown sugar (optional)

¹/₄ teaspoon salt

¹/₄ teaspoon black pepper

Fresh Italian (flat-leaf) parsley leaves

1 In a covered large saucepan cook sweet potatoes in enough boiling water to cover for 10 to 12 minutes or until tender.

2 Meanwhile, in an extra-large nonstick skillet heat oil over medium-high heat. Add onions; cook for 5 minutes. Add sweet peppers; cook about 3 minutes more or until crisp-tender. Add tomatoes, brown sugar (if using), salt, and black pepper. Bring to boiling; reduce heat. Simmer, uncovered, about 5 minutes or until most of the liquid evaporates.

3 Drain the cooked sweet potatoes well. Stir sweet potatoes into the tomato mixture. To serve, sprinkle with parsley leaves.

1 gram fat

PER SERVING: 80 cal., 1 g total fat (0 g sat. fat), 0 mg chol., 221 mg sodium, 16 g carb. (3 g fiber, 7 g sugars), 2 g pro. Exchanges: 1 starch.

Spicy Vegetable Bake

A fresh jalapeño chile pepper adds a touch of heat to the traditional cheesy vegetable bake of carrots, broccoli, and cauliflower.

SERVINGS 10 ($^3/_4$ cup each)
CARB. PER SERVING 15 g
PREP 25 minutes
BAKE 25 minutes

Nonstick cooking spray

1 tablespoon butter

1 tablespoon olive oil

3 tablespoons flour

1$^1/_4$ cups fat-free milk

7 Individually wrapped slices 2% milk cheddar cheese (about 4$^1/_2$ ounces total), torn into bite-size pieces

1 medium fresh jalapeño chile pepper, thinly sliced*

$^1/_2$ teaspoon salt

Freshly ground black pepper (optional)

1 16-ounce package peeled fresh baby carrots

3 cups broccoli florets

3 cups cauliflower florets

1 8-ounce can sliced water chestnuts, drained

$^1/_2$ cup whole wheat panko (Japanese-style bread crumbs)

PER SERVING: 126 cal., 5 g total fat (2 g sat. fat), 11 mg chol., 374 mg sodium, 15 g carb. (3 g fiber, 6 g sugars), 6 g pro. Exchanges: 0.5 milk, 2 vegetable, 0.5 fat.

1 Preheat oven to 375°F. Lightly coat a 2-quart oval or rectangular baking dish with cooking spray; set aside.

2 For cheese sauce, in a medium saucepan melt butter over medium heat. Add oil. Whisk in flour until dissolved. Whisk in milk. Cook and whisk until thickened and bubbly. Add torn cheese slices; cook and stir until cheese melts. Remove from heat. Stir in sliced chile pepper, salt, and, if desired, black pepper.

3 In a Dutch oven bring 5 cups water to boiling. Add carrots; cook for 4 minutes (water may not return to boiling). Add broccoli and cauliflower. Cook, uncovered, for 4 minutes more. Drain in a colander set in a sink. In the Dutch oven combine vegetables and water chestnuts. Spoon into the prepared baking dish. Top with the cheese sauce. Sprinkle panko on top of the vegetables; coat with cooking spray.

4 Bake for 25 to 30 minutes or until vegetables are crisp-tender, cheese sauce is bubbly, and topping is golden brown.

*TEST KITCHEN TIP: Because chile peppers contain volatile oils that can burn your skin and eyes, avoid direct contact with them as much as possible. When working with chile peppers, wear plastic or rubber gloves. If your bare hands do touch the peppers, wash your hands and nails well with soap and warm water. For a milder dish, remove membranes and seeds from the chile pepper.

Root Vegetable Puree

Here's a great way to slide a few more vegetables into your family's diet. Slightly sweet rutabaga is delicious when mashed with potatoes.

SERVINGS 8 (¹/₂ cup each)
CARB. PER SERVING 12 g
START TO FINISH 35 minutes

1 pound Yukon gold potatoes, peeled and cut into 2-inch pieces

1 pound rutabaga, peeled and cut into 2-inch pieces

2 tablespoons light butter or light tub-style vegetable oil spread

¼ teaspoon salt

¼ teaspoon black pepper

¼ to ¹/₃ cup fat-free milk

1 cup coarsely chopped fresh spinach

1 recipe Porcini-Rubbed Roast Beef *(page 71)* (optional)

1 In a large saucepan cook potatoes and rutabaga, covered, in enough boiling water to cover about 20 minutes or until vegetables are tender; drain.

2 Mash potatoes and rutabaga with a potato masher or beat with an electric mixer on low speed. Add butter, salt, and pepper. Gradually beat in enough milk to make mixture light and fluffy. Stir in spinach just before serving. If desired, serve with Porcini Rubbed Roast Beef.

PER SERVING: 67 cal., 2 g total fat (1 g sat. fat), 4 mg chol., 112 mg sodium, 12 g carb. (2 g fiber, 3 g sugars), 2 g pro. Exchanges: 1 starch.

12 grams carb

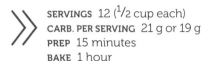

Corn Casserole

A holiday meal wouldn't be the same without corn casserole. This version is made with good-for-you ingredients and will fit a diabetes meal plan.

SERVINGS 12 ($^1/_2$ cup each)
CARB. PER SERVING 21 g or 19 g
PREP 15 minutes
BAKE 1 hour

Nonstick cooking spray

30 saltine crackers, crushed (about 1 cup)

2 tablespoons sugar*

$^1/_4$ teaspoon salt

$^1/_4$ teaspoon black pepper

2 cups fat-free milk

$^3/_4$ cup refrigerated or frozen egg product, thawed

2 tablespoons butter, melted

4 cups frozen whole kernel corn

Snipped fresh parsley (optional)

1 Preheat oven to 325°F. Generously coat a 2-quart rectangular baking dish with cooking spray; set aside.

2 In a large bowl combine crushed crackers, sugar, salt, and pepper. Stir in milk, egg, and melted butter. Stir in frozen corn.

3 Pour corn mixture into the prepared baking dish. Bake for 1 to 1$^1/_4$ hours or until a knife inserted near the center comes out clean. If desired, sprinkle with parsley.

***SUGAR SUBSTITUTES:** Choose from Splenda Granular or Sweet'N Low bulk or packets. Follow package directions to use product amount equivalent to 2 tablespoons sugar.

PER SERVING: 119 cal., 3 g total fat (1 g sat. fat), 6 mg chol., 233 mg sodium, 21 g carb. (1 g fiber, 6 g sugars), 5 g pro. Exchanges: 1 starch, 0.5 carb., 0.5 fat.

PER SERVING WITH SUBSTITUTE: Same as above, except 112 cal., 19 g carb. (4 g sugars). Exchanges: 0 carb.

Date- and Balsamic-Glazed Brussels Sprouts

Chopping dates can be sticky business, so coat the chef's knife with nonstick cooking spray before the chopping begins.

SERVINGS 8 ($^3/_4$ cup each)
CARB. PER SERVING 17 g
PREP 25 minutes
ROAST 20 minutes

- 2 pounds fresh Brussels sprouts
- 1 tablespoon olive oil
- 2 teaspoons butter
- 3 cloves garlic, minced
- $^1/_3$ cup balsamic vinegar
- $^1/_4$ cup pitted whole dates, chopped
- $^1/_4$ teaspoon salt
- $^1/_8$ teaspoon black pepper

1 Preheat oven to 425°F. Trim stems and remove any wilted outer leaves from Brussels sprouts; wash. Halve Brussels sprouts; spread in a single layer in a 15×10×1-inch baking pan. Drizzle oil over Brussels sprouts. Roast for 20 to 25 minutes or until crisp-tender, stirring once or twice.

2 Meanwhile, for sauce, in a large nonstick skillet melt butter over medium heat. Add garlic; cook for 30 seconds. Add balsamic vinegar, dates, salt, and pepper. Cook for 5 to 7 minutes or until sauce is thickened and reduced to about $^1/_4$ cup.

3 Add roasted Brussels sprouts to the sauce in skillet; stir to coat.

PER SERVING: 99 cal., 3 g total fat (1 g sat. fat), 3 mg chol., 112 mg sodium, 17 g carb. (5 g fiber, 8 g sugars), 4 g pro. Exchanges: 2 vegetable, 0.5 fruit, 0.5 fat.

Steamed Artichokes with Caramelized Onion Aïoli

Pretty on a plate and fun to eat, whole artichokes make great holiday finger food. They pair well with fish and seafood.

SERVINGS 4 (1 small artichoke and 8 teaspoons aïoli each)
CARB. PER SERVING 15 g
PREP 25 minutes
COOK 20 minutes

4   small artichokes

½   teaspoon finely shredded lemon peel (set aside)

4   teaspoons lemon juice

Nonstick cooking spray

1   cup chopped onion

2   cloves garlic, minced

¼   cup light mayonnaise

¼   cup finely shredded Parmesan cheese

2   tablespoons snipped fresh Italian (flat-leaf) parsley

Freshly ground black pepper

PER SERVING: 117 cal., 5 g total fat (1 g sat. fat), 6 mg chol., 280 mg sodium, 15 g carb. (5 g fiber, 3 g sugars), 5 g pro. Exchanges: 3 vegetable, 1 fat.

1 | Wash artichokes; trim stems and remove loose outer leaves. Cut off 1 inch from each artichoke top; snip off the sharp leaf tips. Brush cut edges with 1 teaspoon of the lemon juice. In a Dutch oven bring a large amount of water to boiling; add artichokes. Return to boiling; reduce heat. Simmer, covered, for 20 to 30 minutes or until a leaf comes out easily when carefully pulled.

2 | Meanwhile, for aïoli, coat an unheated medium nonstick skillet with cooking spray; heat over medium heat. Add onion. Cover and cook about 10 minutes or until onion is golden brown, stirring occasionally. Add garlic; cook and stir for 30 seconds.

3 | Transfer onion mixture to a blender. Add remaining 3 teaspoons lemon juice and the mayonnaise. Cover and blend until almost smooth. Transfer onion mixture to a small bowl. Stir in lemon peel, cheese, and half of the parsley until well combined. Divide mixture among four small serving cups. Sprinkle evenly with remaining parsley and freshly ground pepper.

4 | Drain artichokes upside down on paper towels. Serve drained artichokes with aïoli.*

*TEST KITCHEN TIP: To eat an artichoke, pull off a leaf and dip the leaf base in the aïoli. Draw the leaf base through your teeth, scraping off only tender flesh. Discard remainder of leaf. Continue removing leaves until fuzzy choke appears. Scoop out choke with a grapefruit spoon and discard. Eat the remaining heart with a fork, dipping each piece into aïoli.

Chorizo Custard Dressing

Big flavor comes from a little Spanish-style chorizo in this soft dressing. If you wish, garnish each serving with a snippet of fresh thyme.

SERVINGS 8 (1 ramekin each)
CARB. PER SERVING 10 g
PREP 15 minutes
BAKE 25 minutes
STAND 10 minutes

3	ounces whole grain baguette-style French bread
4	ounces cooked Spanish-style chorizo, chopped
2	ounces Manchego cheese, shredded
½	cup bottled roasted red sweet peppers, drained and chopped
½	cup thinly sliced green onions (4)
1¼	cups refrigerated or frozen egg product, thawed, or 5 eggs, lightly beaten
1	cup fat-free milk
½	cup fat-free half-and-half
1	recipe Lemon-Thyme Spiraled Pork Loin (page 69) (optional)

PER SERVING: 166 cal., 9 g total fat (3 g sat. fat), 126 mg chol., 432 mg sodium, 10 g carb. (1 g fiber, 4 g sugars), 12 g pro. Exchanges: 0.5 starch, 1.5 lean meat, 1 fat.

1 Preheat oven to 350°F. Tear bread into large pieces and place in a food processor. Cover and pulse with several on-off turns to make coarse crumbs. Transfer crumbs to a medium bowl and stir in chorizo, cheese, sweet peppers, and green onions. Spoon mixture evenly into eight 6- to 8-ounce ramekins.

2 In another medium bowl whisk together eggs, milk, and half-and-half. Slowly and evenly pour over bread mixture in ramekins. Using the back of a large spoon, press down lightly on the bread mixture so all the bread is moistened with egg mixture. Place ramekins in a 15×10×1-inch baking pan.

3 Bake for 25 to 30 minutes or until a knife inserted in centers of ramekins comes out clean. Let stand for 10 minutes before serving in the ramekins. If desired, serve with Lemon-Thyme Spiraled Pork Loin.

Clementine-Arugula Salad with Lime-Poppy Seed Dressing

Clementines are easy to peel and section, but if you don't have any on hand, substitute canned mandarin orange sections.

SERVINGS 8 (1¼ cups each)
CARB. PER SERVING 14 g or 12 g
START TO FINISH 35 minutes

¼ cup lime juice

2 tablespoons olive oil

1 tablespoon sugar*

2 teaspoons poppy seeds

⅛ teaspoon kosher salt

⅛ teaspoon freshly ground black pepper

10 cups arugula or baby arugula

8 seedless clementines, peeled and broken into segments

¼ cup chopped walnuts, toasted

¼ cup pomegranate seeds**

1 For dressing, in a screw-top jar combine lime juice, oil, sugar, poppy seeds, kosher salt, and pepper. Cover and shake well.

2 In a large salad bowl toss dressing with arugula. Add clementine segments; gently toss. Divide among eight salad plates. Sprinkle with walnuts and pomegranate seeds.

*SUGAR SUBSTITUTES: Choose from Splenda Granular, Equal Spoonful or packets, or Sweet'N Low bulk or packets. Follow package directions to use product amount equivalent to 1 tablespoon sugar.

**TEST KITCHEN TIP: To prepare pomegranate seeds, score an "X" in the top of a pomegranate. Break pomegranate apart into quarters. Working in a bowl of cool water, immerse each quarter; use your fingers to loosen the seeds from the white membrane. Discard peel and membrane. Drain seeds. Cover and chill for up to 24 hours before using.

PER SERVING: 110 cal., 6 g total fat (1 g sat. fat), 0 mg chol., 39 mg sodium, 14 g carb. (2 g fiber, 10 g sugars), 2 g pro. Exchanges: 1 fruit, 1 fat.

PER SERVING WITH SUBSTITUTE: Same as above, except 105 cal., 12 g carb. (8 g sugars).

QUICK TIP
If arugula is too piquant for your taste, mix together equal parts of baby spinach and arugula. Or substitute mixed baby greens for the arugula.

Sweet-Tart Winter Salad

A spoonful of sweet honey helps balance the tart grapefruit. Although pink grapefruit appear more festive, white grapefruit can be used, too.

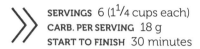

SERVINGS 6 (1¼ cups each)
CARB. PER SERVING 18 g
START TO FINISH 30 minutes

9 cups torn butterhead (Boston or Bibb) lettuce

2 cups pink grapefruit sections* (set aside)

¼ cup grapefruit juice reserved from sectioning grapefruit

1½ tablespoons olive oil

1 tablespoon honey

¼ teaspoon salt

¼ teaspoon cracked black pepper

6 small shallots, thinly sliced and separated into rings

2 ounces Parmesan cheese, coarsely shredded

1 | Divide lettuce among six salad plates. Set aside.

2 | For dressing, in a medium bowl whisk together the ¼ cup reserved grapefruit juice, the olive oil, honey, salt, and pepper. Toss grapefruit sections with dressing; arrange on top of lettuce on salad plates. Top with shallots and Parmesan cheese.

*TEST KITCHEN TIP: To section grapefruit, work over a bowl to catch juice; cut into the center of the grapefruit, cutting between one section and membrane. Cut along the other side of the section next to the membrane to free the section. Repeat with the remaining sections.

6 grams protein

PER SERVING: 139 cal., 6 g total fat (2 g sat. fat), 6 mg chol., 255 mg sodium, 18 g carb. (3 g fiber, 11 g sugars), 6 g pro. Exchanges: 1 vegetable, 1 fruit, 1 fat.

Hearts of Romaine with Creamy Feta Dressing

This knife-and-fork salad goes well with succulent medium-rare beef tenderloin or leg of lamb.

SERVINGS 12 (1 quarter romaine heart and 1 tablespoon dressing each)
CARB. PER SERVING 2 g
START TO FINISH 15 minutes

3 hearts of romaine lettuce
¼ cup water
¼ cup olive oil
2 tablespoons lemon juice
1 tablespoon red wine vinegar
½ cup crumbled feta cheese (2 ounces)
1 teaspoon dried oregano, crushed
1 clove garlic, minced
¼ teaspoon sea salt
¼ teaspoon cayenne pepper
¼ cup crumbled feta cheese (1 ounce)

PER SERVING: 65 cal., 6 g total fat (2 g sat. fat), 6 mg chol., 130 mg sodium, 2 g carb. (1 g fiber, 1 g sugars), 1 g pro. Exchanges: 1 vegetable, 1 fat.

1 Cut each heart of romaine in half lengthwise. Arrange romaine on a serving platter.

2 For dressing, in a food processor or blender combine the water, oil, lemon juice, red wine vinegar, ½ cup cheese, oregano, garlic, and salt. Cover and process or blend until smooth.

3 Drizzle dressing over romaine; sprinkle with cayenne pepper. Top with ¼ cup cheese. To serve, cut romaine halves crosswise into quarters.

Fresh Asparagus Ribbon Salad

Use a vegetable peeler to shave thick asparagus spears into thin ribbons.

SERVINGS 6 (1¾ cups salad and 1 tablespoon dressing each)
CARB. PER SERVING 4 g
START TO FINISH 30 minutes

- 1 pound thick green, purple, and/or white asparagus (about 14 spears)
- 2 cloves garlic, peeled
- ½ teaspoon coarse kosher salt
- ½ cup sour cream
- ⅓ cup olive oil
- 3 to 4 tablespoons lemon juice
- ½ cup chopped fresh Italian (flat-leaf) parsley
- ¼ cup chopped fresh chives
- 1 tablespoon milk (optional)
- Black pepper
- 1 head Bibb lettuce, torn (6 cups)
- ½ of an English (seedless) cucumber, thinly sliced
- 3 radishes, very thinly sliced

PER SERVING: 73 cal., 6 g total fat (1 g sat. fat), 3 mg chol., 73 mg sodium, 4 g carb. (2 g fiber, 2 g sugars), 2 g pro. Exchanges: 1 vegetable, 1 fat.

1 Remove scales from asparagus spears. (The dark triangular leaves or scales on asparagus spears can be especially tough on thick spears. To remove them, use a paring knife to peel them off. Discard the scales.) Using a vegetable peeler, peel thin "ribbons" from the asparagus spears.* For crisp ribbons, place ribbons in a medium bowl of ice water; set aside.

2 Meanwhile, for dressing, make a garlic paste on a cutting board by finely chopping the garlic. Sprinkle with coarse salt. Holding a large flat chef's knife at a slight angle, blade almost flat with cutting board, mash and rub the salt into the garlic.

3 In a bowl whisk together the garlic paste, sour cream, olive oil, and lemon juice. Stir in parsley and chives. If desired, thin with milk. Season to taste with black pepper.

4 Drain asparagus ribbons and pat dry (or spin in a salad spinner). On a platter arrange lettuce, asparagus ribbons and tips, cucumber slices, and radish slices. Drizzle with about 6 tablespoons of the dressing and serve immediately. Cover and refrigerate remaining dressing for up to 3 days. Stir well before serving.

***TEST KITCHEN TIP:** Thin asparagus ribbons are easy to cut using a sharp vegetable peeler on thick asparagus spears. Trim the asparagus, then lay it flat on a work surface. Beginning from the stem or bottom end, peel toward the tips. Either take care to avoid snapping off the tender tips with the peeler or deliberately break off the tips to toss in the salad with the ribbons.

Harvest Slaw

Fresh cilantro leaves add bright flavor to this autumn combo of cabbage, apples, dried cranberries, and pecans.

SERVINGS 12 (³/4 cup each)
CARB. PER SERVING 13 g
START TO FINISH 30 minutes

- 3 tablespoons olive oil
- 2 cloves garlic, coarsely chopped
- 2 teaspoons caraway seeds, lightly crushed
- ¼ cup cider vinegar
- 1 tablespoon honey
- ¼ teaspoon salt
- ¼ teaspoon black pepper
- 4 cups finely shredded red cabbage (or mix red and green)
- 2 red apples, cored and thinly sliced
- ½ cup dried cranberries
- ½ cup pecan halves, toasted
- 2 tablespoons fresh cilantro or parsley leaves

1 In a large skillet heat olive oil over medium heat. Add garlic and caraway seeds; cook and stir for 1 minute. Whisk in vinegar and honey; bring to a simmer. Season with the salt and pepper.

2 In a large bowl toss together the cabbage, apples, cranberries, and pecans. Add dressing and toss to combine. Top with cilantro.

QUICK TIP
To finely shred the cabbage, use a chef's knife to cut it in half. Then cut into thin shreds, separating the shreds as you measure; transfer them to a bowl.

PER SERVING: 105 cal., 7 g total fat (1 g sat. fat), 0 mg chol., 56 mg sodium, 13 g carb. (2 g fiber, 9 g sugars), 1 g pro. Exchanges: 1 vegetable, 0.5 fruit, 1 fat.

13 grams carb

6

fresh-baked
breads

Whatever their form—fancy loaves, knotted rolls, pull-apart

sticks, crown-topped muffins, or flaky scones—fresh-from-the-

oven breads bring oohs and ahhs. Share the wholesomeness

this holiday when you pass a basketful of these specialties

around the table or package some for a heart-warming gift.

Spicy Breadsticks with Bacon

To twist or not to twist? Either way, these golden-brown beauties are filled with bits of bacon and topped with flecks of crushed red pepper.

SERVINGS 48 (1 breadstick each)
CARB. PER SERVING 8 g
PREP 25 minutes
RISE 1 hour 30 minutes
BAKE 10 minutes per batch

2½ to 3 cups all-purpose flour
1 package active dry yeast
1¼ cups fat-free milk
2 tablespoons canola oil
2 tablespoons honey
1 teaspoon salt
½ cup refrigerated or frozen egg product, thawed
¾ cup whole wheat flour
6 slices turkey bacon, crisp-cooked and finely chopped
1 tablespoon water
1 teaspoon crushed red pepper

PER SERVING: 48 cal., 1 g total fat (0 g sat. fat), 1 mg chol., 88 mg sodium, 8 g carb. (0 g fiber, 1 g sugars), 2 g pro. Exchanges: 0.5 starch.

1 In a large mixing bowl combine 1½ cups of the all-purpose flour and the yeast; set aside. In a small saucepan heat and stir milk, oil, honey, and salt over medium heat until warm (120°F to 130°F). Add to flour mixture along with ¼ cup of the egg. Beat with an electric mixer on low speed for 30 seconds, scraping sides of bowl constantly. Beat on high speed for 3 minutes. Using a wooden spoon, stir in the whole wheat flour, bacon, and as much of the remaining all-purpose flour as you can.

2 Turn dough out onto a lightly floured surface. Knead in enough of the remaining all-purpose flour to make a soft dough that is smooth and elastic (3 to 5 minutes total). Shape dough into a ball. Place in a lightly greased bowl, turning once to grease surface of dough. Cover and let rise in a warm place until double in size (about 1 hour).

3 Punch dough down. Turn dough out onto a lightly floured surface; cover and let rest for 10 minutes. Meanwhile, line two large baking sheets with foil; grease foil and set aside.

4 On the lightly floured surface roll dough into a 12×10-inch rectangle. Cut rectangle in half lengthwise. Cut each rectangle crosswise into twenty-four ½-inch-wide strips that are 5 inches long. Twist each dough strip a few times if desired. Place strips on prepared baking sheets, leaving 1 inch between strips. Cover and let rise in a warm place until nearly double in size (about 30 minutes).

5 Preheat oven to 425°F. In a small bowl combine remaining ¼ cup egg and the 1 tablespoon water. Beat with a fork until lightly beaten. Brush lightly over breadsticks. Sprinkle breadsticks with the crushed red pepper.

6 Bake breadsticks, one pan at a time, about 10 minutes or until breadsticks are lightly browned. Transfer breadsticks to wire racks and cool slightly before serving.

TO STORE: Store breadsticks in an airtight container in the refrigerator within 2 hours after baking. If chilled, let stand at room temperature about 30 minutes before serving.

Pull-Apart Cornmeal Dinner Rolls

Perfect for the holiday, this big batch of soft and tender rolls bakes on one baking sheet in just 12 minutes.

SERVINGS 32 (1 roll each)
CARB. PER SERVING 14 g or 13 g
PREP 30 minutes
RISE 1 hour 30 minutes
BAKE 12 minutes
STAND 10 minutes

1 cup milk
$\frac{1}{4}$ cup sugar*
$\frac{1}{4}$ cup butter, cut up
$\frac{1}{4}$ cup yellow cornmeal
1 teaspoon salt
1 package active dry yeast
$\frac{1}{4}$ cup warm water (105°F to 115°F)
1 egg, lightly beaten
$3\frac{3}{4}$ to $4\frac{1}{4}$ cups flour
2 tablespoons butter, melted
1 to 2 tablespoons yellow cornmeal

1 In a small saucepan heat and stir milk, sugar, the $\frac{1}{4}$ cup butter, $\frac{1}{4}$ cup cornmeal, and the salt just until warm (105°F to 115°F) and butter almost melts. In large bowl dissolve yeast in the warm water. Add egg and warm milk mixture. Using a wooden spoon, stir in enough flour to make a soft dough.

2 Turn dough out onto a lightly floured surface. Knead in enough of the remaining flour to make a moderately soft dough that is smooth and elastic (about 3 minutes total). Shape dough into a ball. Place in a lightly greased large bowl, turning once to grease surface of dough. Cover; let rise in a warm place until double in size (about 1 hour).

3 Punch dough down. Turn dough out onto a lightly floured surface. Cover and let rest for 10 minutes. Meanwhile, grease a 15×10×1-inch baking pan.

4 Roll or pat dough into a 10×8-inch rectangle. Cut into $2\frac{1}{2}$×1-inch strips. Arrange strips in prepared pan, leaving about $\frac{1}{4}$ inch between each strip. Cover; let rise in warm place until nearly double in size (about 30 minutes).

5 Preheat oven to 400°F. Brush rolls with the 2 tablespoons melted butter. Sprinkle with 1 to 2 tablespoons cornmeal. Bake for 12 to 15 minutes or until tops are golden brown. Cool slightly. Remove from pan and serve while warm.

PARMESAN-HERB DINNER ROLLS: Prepare as above, except add $\frac{1}{2}$ teaspoon dried rosemary, crushed, or 1 teaspoon dried thyme or oregano, crushed, to the saucepan with the milk mixture. Brush rolls with the butter and sprinkle with 2 tablespoons grated Parmesan cheese instead of the cornmeal. Bake as above.

MAKE-AHEAD DIRECTIONS: Prepare as above through Step 4, except do not let rolls rise in the pan. Cover pan and refrigerate for up to 24 hours. Let rolls stand at room temperature for 30 minutes before baking. Bake as above.

*SUGAR SUBSTITUTE: Use Splenda Sugar Blend. Follow package directions to use product amount equivalent to $\frac{1}{4}$ cup sugar.

PER SERVING: 90 cal., 3 g total fat (2 g sat. fat), 12 mg chol., 98 mg sodium, 14 g carb. (1 g fiber, 2 g sugars), 2 g pro. Exchanges: 1 starch, 0.5 fat.

PER SERVING PARMESAN HERB: Same as above, except 91 cal., 103 mg sodium.

PER SERVING WITH SUBSTITUTE (Plain and Parmesan variation): Same as above, except 88 cal., 13 g carb. (1 g sugars).

Olive-Stuffed Almond Butterhorns

Chop the almond slices before sprinkling them over the rolls.

SERVINGS 20 (1 roll each)
CARB. PER SERVING 21 g
PREP 40 minutes
RISE 1 hour 30 minutes
BAKE 14 minutes

1 package active dry yeast

¼ cup warm water (105°F to 115°F)

1 cup fat-free milk

2 tablespoons olive oil

2 tablespoons honey

¾ teaspoon salt

¼ cup refrigerated or frozen egg product, thawed, or 1 egg, lightly beaten

¾ cup whole wheat flour or white whole wheat flour

½ cup finely chopped, toasted sliced almonds

2¾ to 3¼ cups all-purpose flour

¾ cup finely chopped, pitted mixed olives (such as green, Kalamata, or ripe)

½ cup bottled roasted red sweet peppers, drained, finely chopped, and patted dry on paper towels

3 tablespoons snipped fresh basil

¼ teaspoon freshly ground black pepper

2 tablespoons refrigerated or frozen egg product, thawed, or 1 egg white, lightly beaten

½ cup sliced almonds, chopped

PER SERVING: 141 cal., 5 g total fat (1 g sat. fat), 0 mg chol., 139 mg sodium, 21 g carb. (2 g fiber, 3 g sugars), 5 g pro. Exchanges: 1.5 starch, 1 fat.

1 In a large bowl dissolve yeast in the warm water. In a small saucepan stir together milk, oil, honey, and salt; heat until warm (105°F to 115°F). Add ¼ cup egg and the milk mixture to yeast mixture. Stir in whole wheat flour and chopped, toasted almonds. Gradually stir in enough of the all-purpose flour to make a soft dough.

2 Turn dough out onto lightly floured surface; knead gently for 2 to 3 minutes to make a smooth ball. Knead in just enough of the remaining flour so dough is no longer sticky. Place in a greased large bowl, turning once to grease surface of dough. Cover; let rise in a warm place until double in size (about 1 hour).

3 Punch dough down. Turn dough out onto a lightly floured surface. Divide dough in half; shape each half into a ball. Cover and let rest for 10 minutes. Line two baking sheets with parchment paper; set aside.

4 Meanwhile, in a small bowl combine olives, sweet peppers, basil, and black pepper.

5 On a lightly floured surface roll each dough portion into a 10-inch circle. Cut each dough circle into 10 wedges. Spoon olive mixture evenly on top of dough wedges, spreading it into an even layer over each wedge. To shape, begin at the wide end of each wedge and loosely roll toward the point. Place, point sides down, 2 to 3 inches apart on prepared baking sheets. Cover and let rise until nearly double in size (about 30 minutes).

6 Preheat oven to 375°F. Lightly brush tops of rolls with 2 tablespoons egg and sprinkle tops with ½ cup sliced almonds. Bake rolls for 14 to 16 minutes or until golden brown. Transfer rolls to wire racks. Serve while warm or cool.

QUICK TIP
Once it's out of the oven, immediately remove the bread from the pan so the crust stays dry and crispy instead of getting wet and soggy.

Roasted Garlic and Mushroom Batter Bread

Be sure to finely chop the fresh mushrooms so they are evenly dispersed throughout the bread and fill each yummy bite.

SERVINGS 12 (1 slice each)
CARB. PER SERVING 22 g or 20 g
PREP 30 minutes
ROAST 25 minutes
COOK 5 minutes
RISE 1 hour 30 minutes
BAKE 30 minutes
STAND 10 minutes

1 bulb garlic

1/2 teaspoon olive oil

2 cups finely chopped fresh mushrooms, such as button, cremini, or stemmed shiitake

1 tablespoon olive oil

1/4 cup warm water (105°F to 115°F)

1 package active dry yeast

1 cup low-fat cottage cheese

1/4 cup snipped fresh parsley

1/4 cup refrigerated or frozen egg product, thawed, or 1 egg, lightly beaten

2 tablespoons sugar*

2 tablespoons snipped fresh chives

1/2 teaspoon salt

1/4 teaspoon baking soda

3/4 cup whole wheat flour

1 1/2 to 1 3/4 cups all-purpose flour

PER SERVING: 135 cal., 3 g total fat (0 g sat. fat), 1 mg chol., 213 mg sodium, 22 g carb. (2 g fiber, 3 g sugars), 7 g pro. Exchanges: 1.5 starch, 0.5 lean meat.

PER SERVING WITH SUBSTITUTE: Same as above, except 128 cal., 20 g carb. (1 g sugars).

1 Preheat oven to 425°F. Peel away the dry outer layers of skin from the bulb of garlic, leaving skins and cloves intact. Cut off the pointed top portion (about 1/4 inch), leaving bulb intact but exposing the individual cloves. Place the garlic bulb, cut side up, in a custard cup. Drizzle with 1/2 teaspoon olive oil. Cover cup with foil and roast for 25 to 35 minutes or until the cloves feel soft when pressed. Set aside just until cool enough to handle. Squeeze out the garlic paste from individual cloves and place in a small bowl. Mash with a fork.

2 In a large nonstick skillet cook mushrooms in the 1 tablespoon hot oil over medium heat about 5 minutes or until tender and starting to brown, stirring occasionally. Remove from the heat and set aside.

3 In a large mixing bowl stir together water and yeast. Let stand for 10 minutes. Stir in mushrooms, scraping in as much of the oil from the skillet as possible. Stir in roasted garlic, cottage cheese, parsley, egg, sugar, chives, salt, and baking soda. Stir in the whole wheat flour and enough of the all-purpose flour to make a stiff dough that is still sticky. Transfer dough to a greased bowl, turning once to grease the surface of the dough. Cover and let rise in a warm place until double in size (1 to 1 1/4 hours).

4 Lightly grease the bottom of a 9-inch round baking pan. Line bottom of the pan with parchment paper or waxed paper; grease and lightly flour pan. Set pan aside. Punch dough down. Place dough in the prepared pan. Cover and let rise in a warm place until nearly double in size (30 to 40 minutes).

5 Preheat oven to 350°F. Bake for 30 to 35 minutes or until an instant-read thermometer inserted into center of bread registers 200°F. If necessary, cover the top of the loaf for the last 10 to 15 minutes to prevent overbrowning.

6 Loosen edges of bread from the pan with a thin spatula. Immediately remove the bread from the pan. Peel off waxed paper or parchment paper; cool completely on a wire rack before slicing.

*SUGAR SUBSTITUTES: Choose from Splenda Granular, Truvia Spoonable, or Sweet'N Low bulk or packets. Follow package directions to use product amount equivalent to 2 tablespoons sugar.

Whole Wheat Cranberry Dinner Rolls

Lining the baking sheet with parchment paper makes cleanup easy because the cranberry topping drips onto the sheet as it bakes.

SERVINGS 12 (1 roll each)
CARB. PER SERVING 19 g or 18 g
PREP 20 minutes
RISE 30 minutes
BAKE 18 minutes

- ¼ cup fresh cranberries, chopped
- 1½ teaspoons sugar*
- 2 tablespoons butter, melted
- ½ teaspoon dried thyme, crushed
- ¼ teaspoon ground ginger
- 1 1-pound loaf frozen whole wheat bread dough, thawed

PER SERVING: 118 cal., 3 g total fat (1 g sat. fat), 5 mg chol., 227 mg sodium, 19 g carb. (2 g fiber, 1 g sugars), 5 g pro. Exchanges: 1 starch, 1 fat.

PER SERVING WITH SUBSTITUTE: Same as above, except 116 cal., 18 g carb. (0 g sugars).

1 In a small bowl combine cranberries and sugar. Stir in 1 tablespoon of the melted butter, ¼ teaspoon of the thyme, and the ginger.

2 Line a baking sheet with parchment paper. Dust work surface lightly with flour. Divide dough into 12 equal pieces. Roll each piece of dough into a 12-inch-long rope. Tie each dough rope into a loose knot, leaving two long ends. Tuck top end under knot and bottom end into top center of the knot. Place knots 2 to 3 inches apart on prepared baking sheet. Spoon 1 teaspoon of the cranberry mixture into the center of each knot. Cover and let rise in a warm place until nearly double in size (30 to 60 minutes).

3 Preheat oven to 350°F. In a small bowl stir together the remaining 1 tablespoon melted butter and the remaining ¼ teaspoon thyme. Brush butter-thyme mixture over tops of rolls. Bake about 18 minutes or until golden brown.

*SUGAR SUBSTITUTES: Choose from Splenda Granular or Truvia Spoonable Sweetener. Follow package directions to use product amount equivalent to 1½ teaspoons sugar.

Whole Wheat Pumpkin Bread

This lightened-up version has 78 fewer calories and 5 g less fat per serving than classic pumpkin bread.

SERVINGS 32 (1 slice each)
CARB. PER SERVING 21 g
PREP 25 minutes
COOL 10 minutes
BAKE 45 minutes

- ¾ cup granulated sugar*
- ¾ cup packed brown sugar*
- 1 6-ounce carton plain low-fat yogurt
- ¼ cup vegetable oil
- 4 eggs
- 2⅓ cups whole wheat pastry flour or white whole wheat flour
- 1 cup all-purpose flour
- 2 teaspoons baking soda
- 1½ teaspoons salt
- 1½ teaspoons ground cinnamon
- 1 teaspoon ground nutmeg
- ⅔ cup water
- 1 15-ounce can pumpkin

1 Preheat oven to 350°F. Grease the bottom and ½ inch up the sides of two 9x5x3-inch, three 8x4x2-inch, or four 7½x3½x2-inch loaf pans; set aside. In an extra-large bowl beat granulated sugar, brown sugar, yogurt, and oil with an electric mixer on medium speed until combined. Add eggs; beat well.

2 In a large bowl stir together whole wheat pastry flour, all-purpose flour, baking soda, salt, cinnamon, and nutmeg. Alternately add flour mixture and the water to egg mixture, beating on low speed after each addition just until combined. Beat in pumpkin.

3 Spoon batter into the prepared loaf pans; spread evenly. Bake for 45 to 50 minutes for 9x5-inch loaves, 40 to 45 minutes for 8x4-inch loaves, 35 to 40 minutes for 7½x3-inch loaves, or until a toothpick inserted near the centers comes out clean.

4 Cool in pans on wire racks for 10 minutes. Remove from pans. Cool completely on wire racks. Wrap and store overnight before slicing. Cut each 9-inch loaf into 16 slices.

*SUGAR SUBSTITUTES: We do not recommend using a sugar substitute for this recipe.

PER SERVING: 117 cal., 3 g total fat (0 g sat. fat), 24 mg chol., 203 mg sodium, 21 g carb. (2 g fiber, 11 g sugars), 3 g pro. Exchanges: 1 starch, 0.5 carb., 0.5 fat.

3 grams protein

Coconut Apricot Braid

If you wish, substitute dried cranberries or dried cherries for half or all of the dried apricots.

SERVINGS 16 (1 slice each)
CARB. PER SERVING 28 g or 25 g
PREP 40 minutes
RISE 2 hours
BAKE 35 minutes
STAND 10 minutes

2 to 2$\frac{1}{2}$ cups all-purpose flour
1 package active dry yeast
$\frac{1}{2}$ teaspoon ground cardamom
$\frac{3}{4}$ cup coconut water
$\frac{1}{3}$ cup sugar*
$\frac{1}{4}$ cup light butter, cut up
$\frac{1}{2}$ teaspoon salt
$\frac{1}{4}$ cup refrigerated or frozen egg product, thawed, or 1 egg, lightly beaten
$\frac{3}{4}$ cup whole wheat flour
$\frac{1}{2}$ cup chopped dried apricots
$\frac{1}{2}$ cup powdered sugar
2 to 3 teaspoons coconut water
$\frac{1}{4}$ cup flaked coconut, toasted

PER SERVING: 144 cal., 2 g total fat (1 g sat. fat), 4 mg chol., 122 mg sodium, 28 g carb. (2 g fiber, 11 g sugars), 3 g pro. Exchanges: 0.5 fruit, 1 starch, 0.5 carb.

PER SERVING WITH SUBSTITUTE: Same as above, except 129 cal., 25 g carb. (7 g sugars). Exchanges: 0 carb.

1 In a large mixing bowl stir together 1 cup of the all-purpose flour, the yeast, and cardamom. In a medium saucepan heat and stir $\frac{3}{4}$ cup coconut water, the sugar, butter, and salt just until warm (120°F to 130°F) and butter is almost melted. Add to flour mixture along with egg. Beat with an electric mixer on low speed for 30 seconds, scraping sides of bowl constantly. Beat on high speed for 3 minutes. Using a wooden spoon, stir in the whole wheat flour, apricots, and as much of the remaining all-purpose flour as you can.

2 Turn dough out onto a lightly floured surface. Knead in enough of the remaining flour to make a moderately soft dough that is smooth and elastic (3 to 5 minutes). Shape dough into a ball. Place dough in a greased bowl; turn once to grease surface of dough. Cover and let rise in a warm place until double in size (about 1 to 1$\frac{1}{2}$ hours).

3 Punch dough down. Turn dough out onto a lightly floured surface. Divide dough into three portions; cover and let rest for 10 minutes. Meanwhile, lightly grease a large baking sheet.

4 Shape each portion of dough into a 16-inch-long rope. Line up ropes about 1 inch apart on prepared baking sheet. Starting in the middle of the ropes, loosely braid by bringing the left rope under the center rope. Next bring right rope under the new center rope. Repeat to the end. On the other end, braid by bringing alternate ropes over center rope from center to end. Press ends together to seal; tuck under. Cover; let rise in a warm place until nearly double in size (about 1 hour).

5 Preheat oven to 325°F. Bake braid about 35 minutes or until bread sounds hollow when lightly tapped. If necessary to prevent overbrowning, cover loosely with foil during the last 10 to 15 minutes of baking. Immediately remove from baking sheet. Cool on a wire rack.

6 For icing, in a small bowl stir together powdered sugar and 2 to 3 teaspoons coconut water to make a smooth icing that is drizzling consistency. Drizzle over cooled loaf and sprinkle with toasted coconut. Cut loaf into 16 slices.

*SUGAR SUBSTITUTES: Choose from Splenda Granular, Truvia Spoonable, or Sweet'N Low bulk or packets. Follow package directions to use product amount equivalent to $\frac{1}{3}$ cup sugar.

Chocolate Peanut Butter Scones

For bits of chocolate in every bite, use the miniature semisweet chocolate pieces.

SERVINGS 16 (1 scone each)
CARB. PER SERVING 25 g or 23 g
PREP 25 minutes
BAKE 12 minutes

2¼ cups all-purpose flour

½ cup whole wheat pastry flour

¼ cup packed brown sugar*

1 tablespoon baking powder

¼ teaspoon salt

⅓ cup creamy peanut butter

3 tablespoons butter

¾ cup fat-free milk

½ cup refrigerated or frozen egg product, thawed

½ cup semisweet chocolate pieces

1 Preheat oven to 400°F. Lightly grease a large baking sheet; set aside. In a large bowl combine flours, brown sugar, baking powder, and salt. Using a pastry blender, cut in peanut butter and butter until mixture resembles coarse crumbs. Make a well in the center of the flour mixture; set aside.

2 In a small bowl whisk together milk and eggs. Add all at once to flour mixture along with chocolate pieces. Stir until moistened (dough will be sticky).

3 Turn dough out onto a well-floured surface. Knead gently for 10 to 12 strokes or until dough holds together and is smooth. Divide dough in half. Pat each portion into a 6-inch circle. Cut each circle into eight wedges, dipping knife into flour between cuts if necessary. Place wedges 2 inches apart on prepared baking sheet.

4 Bake about 12 minutes or until tops are lightly browned. Transfer scones to a wire rack. Serve while warm.

*SUGAR SUBSTITUTE: Choose Splenda Brown Sugar Blend. Follow package directions to use product amount equivalent to ¼ cup brown sugar.

PER SERVING: 180 cal., 7 g total fat (3 g sat. fat), 6 mg chol., 192 mg sodium, 25 g carb. (1 g fiber, 9 g sugars), 5 g pro. Exchanges: 1 starch, 0.5 carb., 1.5 fat.

PER SERVING WITH SUBSTITUTE: Same as above, except 174 cal., 23 g carb. (7 g sugars), 191 mg sodium.

QUICK TIP

For a grab-and-go breakfast, individually wrap the scones in freezer wrap and freeze for up to 3 months. Grab one on your way out the door, then give it a quick zap in the microwave when you get to the office.

Apple Hazelnut Oat Bread

To toast hazelnuts, spread them in a shallow baking sheet. Bake in a 350°F oven for 8 to 10 minutes or until toasted, stirring twice. Cool slightly. Transfer nuts to a clean kitchen towel and rub with the towel to remove papery skins.

SERVINGS 12 (1 slice each)
CARB. PER SERVING 24 g
PREP 30 minutes
BAKE 40 minutes
COOL 10 minutes

1¼ cups flour

¼ cup rolled oats

⅓ cup packed brown sugar*

1 teaspoon baking powder

1 teaspoon apple pie spice

½ teaspoon baking soda

¼ teaspoon salt

2 egg whites

⅓ cup unsweetened applesauce

3 tablespoons light butter, melted

1 teaspoon vanilla

1 cup shredded red cooking apple

½ cup chopped, toasted hazelnuts

⅓ cup rolled oats

2 tablespoons packed brown sugar*

2 tablespoons light butter, softened

PER SERVING: 157 cal., 6 g total fat (2 g sat. fat), 6 mg chol., 195 mg sodium, 24 g carb. (2 g fiber, 10 g sugars), 3 g pro. Exchanges: 1 starch, 0.5 carb., 1 fat.

1 Preheat oven to 350°F. Grease bottom and ½ inch up the sides of an 8x4x2-inch loaf pan. Set aside.

2 In a large bowl combine flour, ¼ cup oats, ⅓ cup brown sugar, the baking powder, ½ teaspoon of the apple pie spice, the baking soda, and salt.

3 In a bowl combine egg whites, applesauce, melted butter, and vanilla. Add to flour mixture; stir until just moistened. Fold in shredded apple. In a bowl combine hazelnuts, ⅓ cup oats, 2 tablespoons brown sugar, and remaining ½ teaspoon apple pie spice. Use your fingers to work in the 2 tablespoons butter until mixture is crumbly.

4 Spoon half the apple mixture into the prepared pan; spread evenly. Sprinkle with half of the hazelnut mixture. Spoon remaining apple mixture over hazelnut layer; spread evenly. Sprinkle with remaining hazelnut mixture.

5 Bake for 40 to 50 minutes or until a toothpick inserted near center comes out clean. If necessary, cover top loosely with foil for the last 10 to 15 minutes to prevent overbrowning. Cool in pan on wire rack for 10 minutes. Remove bread from pan and cool completely on rack. For easier slicing, wrap and store overnight.

*SUGAR SUBSTITUTES: We do not recommend using a sugar substitute for this recipe.

Cherry-Walnut-Stuffed Monkey Bread

Start with frozen dinner roll dough and end up with soft and chewy little bites of ooey-gooey goodness. To serve, simply pull apart each little ball.

SERVINGS 16 (3 pieces each)
CARB. PER SERVING 28 g or 26 g
PREP 25 minutes
CHILL overnight
BAKE 18 minutes

12 rolls frozen cracked wheat dinner roll dough (½ of a 48-ounce package)

½ cup light maple-flavor syrup

¼ cup packed brown sugar*

2 tablespoons light butter

⅓ cup dried tart cherries, chopped

⅓ cup walnuts, toasted and finely chopped

1 tablespoon finely shredded orange peel

1 teaspoon ground cinnamon

1 | Grease a large baking sheet. Place frozen rolls about 2 inches apart on prepared baking sheet. Cover with plastic wrap. Chill in the refrigerator overnight to let dough thaw and begin to rise.

2 | Preheat oven to 350°F. Generously grease a 10-inch fluted tube pan. In a small saucepan combine syrup, brown sugar, and butter. Heat and stir over medium-low heat just until boiling. Remove from the heat and pour into the prepared pan.

3 | In a small bowl combine cherries, walnuts, orange peel, and cinnamon. Cut each roll into quarters. Using your hands, flatten each piece to about 2 inches in diameter; spoon about ½ teaspoon of the cherry mixture into the center of each piece. Pull edges of dough up around cherry mixture and pinch together to seal cherry mixture inside the dough. Layer filled dough pieces over syrup mixture in the prepared pan.

4 | Bake for 40 to 45 minutes or until rolls are golden-brown. Cool rolls in pan on a wire rack for 1 minute. Loosen rolls from edges and the center post. Invert rolls onto a large serving platter. Scrape any remaining syrup mixture from the pan onto rolls. Cool slightly. Serve while warm.

*SUGAR SUBSTITUTE: Choose Splenda Brown Sugar Blend. Follow package directions to use product amount equivalent to ¼ cup brown sugar.

PER SERVING: 165 cal., 4 g total fat (1 g sat. fat), 2 mg chol., 193 mg sodium, 28 g carb. (3 g fiber, 11 g sugars), 4 g pro. Exchanges: 1.5 starch, 0.5 carb., 0.5 fat.

PER SERVING WITH SUBSTITUTE: Same as above, except 160 cal., 26 g carb. (10 g sugars), 192 mg sodium.

Banana-Fig Ginger Muffins

Unlike flaxseeds, chia seeds do not need to be crushed or ground to unlock their powerful antioxidants and nutrients.

SERVINGS 12 (1 muffin each)
CARB. PER SERVING 30 g or 26 g
PREP 25 minutes
BAKE 18 minutes
COOL 5 minutes

Nonstick cooking spray

1½ cups all-purpose flour

½ cup whole wheat flour

2 teaspoons baking powder

½ teaspoon ground ginger

¼ teaspoon baking soda

¼ teaspoon salt

1 cup mashed ripe bananas (2 to 3 medium)

½ cup fat-free milk

⅓ cup packed brown sugar*

¼ cup refrigerated or frozen egg product, thawed, or 1 egg, lightly beaten

¼ cup canola oil

⅓ cup finely chopped, stemmed dried Mission figs

1 tablespoon finely chopped crystallized ginger

1 tablespoon chia seeds or poppy seeds

PER SERVING: 177 cal., 5 g total fat (0 g sat. fat), 0 mg chol., 173 mg sodium, 30 g carb. (2 g fiber, 11 g sugars), 4 g pro. Exchanges: 0.5 fruit, 1 starch, 0.5 carb., 1 fat.

PER SERVING WITH SUBSTITUTE: Same as above, except 167 cal., 26 g carb. (7 g sugars), 171 mg sodium.

1 Preheat oven to 375°F. Coat twelve 2½-inch muffin cups with cooking spray; set aside. In a large bowl stir together flours, baking powder, ground ginger, baking soda, and salt. Make a well in the center of the flour mixture; set aside.

2 In a medium bowl stir together the mashed bananas, milk, brown sugar, egg, and oil. Add banana mixture all at once to flour mixture. Stir just until moistened (batter should be lumpy). Fold in figs. Spoon batter evenly into prepared muffin cups, filling each about three-fourths full.

3 In a small bowl combine crystallized ginger and chia seeds. Sprinkle evenly over muffins.

4 Bake for 18 to 20 minutes or until a toothpick inserted in the centers of muffins comes out clean. Cool muffins in pans on a wire rack for 5 minutes. Remove muffins from pans. Cool slightly and serve while warm.

*SUGAR SUBSTITUTE: Choose Splenda Brown Sugar Blend. Follow package directions to use product amount equivalent to ⅓ cup brown sugar.

Blueberry Ricotta Muffins

Gently hold each muffin, invert, and dip it into the glaze. Once it's glazed, set each muffin, glaze side up, on a wire rack and let dry.

SERVINGS 16 (1 muffin each)
CARB. PER SERVING 27 g
PREP 15 minutes
BAKE 15 minutes

Nonstick cooking spray

1½ cups all-purpose flour

½ cup oat flour or whole wheat pastry flour

1½ teaspoons baking powder

¼ teaspoon baking soda

¼ teaspoon salt

¾ cup part-skim ricotta cheese

¾ cup fat-free milk

½ cup refrigerated or frozen egg product, thawed, or 2 eggs, lightly beaten

⅓ cup honey

3 tablespoons canola oil

2 teaspoons finely shredded orange peel

1 cup fresh or frozen blueberries*

1 cup powdered sugar

5 to 6 teaspoons orange juice

1 | Preheat oven to 375°F. Coat sixteen 2½-inch muffin cups with cooking spray; set aside. In a medium bowl stir together flours, baking powder, baking soda, and salt. Make a well in the center of the flour mixture; set aside.

2 | In a small bowl stir together ricotta cheese, milk, eggs, honey, oil, and the 2 teaspoons orange peel. Add milk mixture all at once to flour mixture. Stir just until moistened (batter should be lumpy). Fold in blueberries. Spoon batter evenly into prepared muffin cups.

3 | Bake for 15 to 18 minutes or until a wooden toothpick inserted in the centers of muffins comes out clean. Cool muffins in pans on a wire rack for 5 minutes. Remove muffins from pans and cool on a wire rack.

4 | For glaze, in a small bowl combine powdered sugar and orange juice. Whisk until smooth. Dip tops of cooled muffins in the orange glaze. Let stand until glaze is set.

*TEST KITCHEN TIP: If using frozen blueberries, do not thaw the berries before adding to the batter.

4 grams fat

PER SERVING: 157 cal., 4 g total fat (1 g sat. fat), 4 mg chol., 137 mg sodium, 27 g carb. (1 g fiber, 15 g sugars), 4 g pro. Exchanges: 1 starch, 1 carb., 0.5 fat.

festive
endings

Who wants to pass up a decadent dessert that's enrobed in

chocolate or crowned with cream? Indulging in something sweet

is reason to celebrate. These lightened-up holiday desserts let you

count each bite of enjoyment instead of the calories, fat, or carbs.

Red Velvet Cake Roll

You won't miss the classic cooked buttercream frosting. This roll of red features a light and creamy filling.

SERVINGS 10 (1 slice each)
CARB. PER SERVING 24 g or 16 g
PREP 30 minutes
STAND 30 minutes
BAKE 12 minutes
CHILL up to 6 hours

4 eggs

1/3 cup flour

1 tablespoon unsweetened cocoa powder

1 teaspoon baking powder

1/2 teaspoon vanilla

1/3 cup granulated sugar*

1 tablespoon red food coloring

1/2 cup granulated sugar*

Powdered sugar

1 cup frozen light whipped dessert topping, thawed

1/2 cup light sour cream

1/2 teaspoon vanilla

PER SERVING: 144 cal., 4 g total fat (2 g sat. fat), 78 mg chol., 72 mg sodium, 24 g carb. (0 g fiber, 18 g sugars), 3 g pro. Exchanges: 0.5 starch, 1 carb., 1 fat.

PER SERVING WITH SUBSTITUTE: Same as above, except 119 cal., 16 g carb. (10 g sugars). Exchanges: 0.5 carb.

1 | Separate eggs. Allow egg whites and yolks to stand at room temperature for 30 minutes. Meanwhile, grease a 15×10×1-inch baking pan. Line bottom of pan with waxed paper or parchment paper; grease paper. Set pan aside. In a medium bowl sift together flour, cocoa powder, and baking powder; set aside.

2 | Preheat oven to 375°F. In a medium mixing bowl beat egg yolks and 1/2 teaspoon vanilla with an electric mixer on high speed about 5 minutes or until thick and lemon color. Gradually add 1/3 cup granulated sugar, beating on high speed until sugar is almost dissolved. Beat in food coloring.

3 | Thoroughly wash beaters. In another mixing bowl beat egg whites on medium speed until soft peaks form (tips curl). Gradually add 1/2 cup granulated sugar, beating until stiff peaks form (tips stand straight). Fold egg yolk mixture into beaten egg whites. Sprinkle flour mixture over egg mixture; fold in gently just until combined. Spread batter evenly in the prepared baking pan.

4 | Bake for 12 to 15 minutes or until cake springs back when lightly touched. Immediately loosen edges of cake from pan and turn cake out onto a clean kitchen towel sprinkled with powdered sugar. Remove waxed paper. Roll towel and cake into a spiral, starting from a short side of the cake. Cool on a wire rack.

5 | For filling, in a medium bowl fold together dessert topping, sour cream, and 1/2 teaspoon vanilla. Unroll cake; remove towel. Spread cake with filling to within 1 inch of the edges. Roll up cake; trim ends. Cover and chill for up to 6 hours. Just before serving, sprinkle cake with additional powdered sugar before slicing.

*SUGAR SUBSTITUTE: Choose Splenda Sugar Blend for the granulated sugar. Follow package directions to use product amounts equivalent to 1/3 cup and 1/2 cup granulated sugar.

Chocolate Almond Torte with Cherry Syrup

Although this Black Forest-like cake is best served right away, leftovers can be chilled for up to 1 day.

SERVINGS 12 (1 wedge each)
CARB. PER SERVING 25 g or 24 g
PREP 35 minutes
BAKE 10 minutes
COOL 1 hour
CHILL 1 hour

1³/₄ cups sliced almonds, toasted

¹/₄ cup unsweetened cocoa powder

2 tablespoons flour

2¹/₂ teaspoons baking powder

1 cup refrigerated or frozen egg product, thawed, or 4 eggs, lightly beaten

¹/₂ cup sugar*

¹/₂ teaspoon almond extract

1 ounce bittersweet or dark chocolate, grated

2 tablespoons sugar**

2 teaspoons cornstarch

¹/₄ teaspoon ground cinnamon

1 tablespoon light butter

1 20-ounce package frozen unsweetened pitted tart red cherries (4 cups)

2 tablespoons water

1 cup frozen light whipped dessert topping, thawed

PER SERVING: 193 cal., 9 g total fat (2 g sat. fat), 1 mg chol., 151 mg sodium, 25 g carb. (3 g fiber, 17 g sugars), 6 g pro. Exchanges: 1 fruit, 0.5 carb., 1 lean meat, 1 fat.

PER SERVING WITH SUBSTITUTE: Same as above, except 190 cal., 24 g carb. (16 g sugars).

1 Preheat oven to 350°F. Grease and flour two 8x1¹/₂-inch round cake pans. Set pans aside. In a medium bowl combine 1¹/₂ cups of the almonds, the cocoa powder, flour, and baking powder; set aside.

2 In a blender or food processor combine egg, ¹/₂ cup sugar, and the almond extract; cover and blend or process until combined. Add nut mixture and grated chocolate. Cover and blend or process until nearly smooth, scraping sides of container occasionally. Divide batter between the prepared pans, spreading evenly.

3 Bake for 10 to 12 minutes or until a toothpick inserted near the centers comes out clean. Cool cake layers in pans on wire racks for 10 minutes. Remove from pans. Cool completely on wire racks.

4 For cherry syrup, in a small bowl combine the 2 tablespoons sugar, the cornstarch, and cinnamon; set aside. In a large skillet heat butter over medium heat just until melted. Remove from heat. Add cherries, sugar mixture, and water. Return to the heat; cook and stir over medium heat until mixture is thickened and bubbly. Cook and stir for 2 minutes more. Remove from heat. Transfer to a large bowl. Cover and cool for 1 hour. Chill for 1 hour before assembling.

5 Just before serving, place one of the cake layers on a serving plate. Spread with whipped dessert topping and half of the cherry syrup. Top with remaining cake layer and remaining syrup. Sprinkle with remaining ¹/₄ cup sliced almonds.

*SUGAR SUBSTITUTES: We do not recommend using a sugar substitute in the cake portion of this recipe.

**SUGAR SUBSTITUTE: Choose Splenda Sugar Blend for Baking for the cherry syrup. Follow package directions to use product amount equivalent to 2 tablespoons sugar.

Carrot Cupcakes

Top each cupcake with a spoonful of frosting and then carefully spread, leaving a rim of cake showing.

SERVINGS 15 (1 cupcake each)
CARB. PER SERVING 30 g or 24 g
PREP 30 minutes
BAKE 18 minutes
COOL 5 minutes

Nonstick cooking spray

 1 cup all-purpose flour

 1 cup whole wheat flour

 3/4 cup packed brown sugar*

 1 teaspoon baking powder

 1 teaspoon baking soda

 3/4 teaspoon ground cinnamon

 1/4 teaspoon salt

 1/4 teaspoon ground ginger

 2 eggs, lightly beaten

 2 cups shredded carrots (4 medium)

 1 cup unsweetened applesauce

 1/3 cup canola oil

 6 ounces reduced-fat cream cheese (Neufchâtel)

 3 tablespoons agave nectar or honey

 5 tablespoons finely shredded carrot

PER SERVING: 207 cal., 8 g total fat (2 g sat. fat), 37 mg chol., 218 mg sodium, 30 g carb. (2 g fiber, 17 g sugars), 4 g pro. Exchanges: 2 starch, 1 fat.

PER SERVING WITH SUBSTITUTE: Same as above, except 189 cal., 215 mg sodium, 24 g carb. (11 g sugars). Exchanges: 1.5 starch.

1 | Preheat oven to 350°F. Line fifteen 2½-inch muffin cups with paper bake cups. Lightly coat paper cups with cooking spray; set aside.

2 | In a large bowl stir together flours, brown sugar, baking powder, baking soda, cinnamon, salt, and ginger; set aside.

3 | In a medium bowl combine eggs, 2 cups carrots, applesauce, and oil. Add egg mixture to flour mixture. Stir until combined. Spoon batter into the prepared muffin cups, filling each three-fourths full.

4 | Bake for 18 to 20 minutes or until a toothpick inserted near centers comes out clean. Cool in muffin cups on a wire rack for 5 minutes. Remove from muffin cups. Cool completely on wire rack.

5 | For frosting, in a small bowl beat cream cheese with an electric mixer on medium speed until smooth. Add agave nectar; beat for 1 minute more. Spread frosting on cupcakes. Top each cupcake with 1 teaspoon of the finely shredded carrots.

SUGAR SUBSTITUTE: Choose Splenda Brown Sugar Blend. Follow package directions to use product amount equivalent to ¾ cup brown sugar.

Raspberry Mocha Ice Cream Brownie Cake

This cake is thick and frozen, so use a long cake knife, bread knife, or chef's knife to cut it into wedges.

SERVINGS 12 (1 wedge each)
CARB. PER SERVING 33 g or 30 g
PREP 30 minutes
BAKE 26 minutes
FREEZE 8 hours

Nonstick cooking spray

1   12- to 13-ounce package sugar-free brownie mix

2   egg whites

1/3   cup canola oil

3   tablespoons water

2   cups chocolate or vanilla no-sugar-added ice cream

4   teaspoons instant coffee crystals

1 1/2   cups frozen unsweetened raspberries, thawed

3   tablespoons sugar*

2   teaspoons cornstarch

2   teaspoons sugar-free chocolate-flavor syrup (optional)

12   fresh raspberries (optional)

1 Preheat oven to 325°F. Coat a 9-inch springform pan with cooking spray; set aside. In a medium bowl combine brownie mix, egg whites, oil, and the water. Mix according to package directions. Spoon batter into the prepared pan. Bake about 26 minutes or until a toothpick inserted 2 inches from the edge comes out clean. Cool in pan on a wire rack. Place pan in freezer and freeze brownie layer for 2 hours.

2 Place ice cream in a chilled medium bowl. Working quickly, stir ice cream to soften; fold in coffee crystals. Spread ice cream evenly over brownie. Cover with plastic wrap. Freeze for at least 8 hours or until very firm.

3 For raspberry sauce, in a small saucepan combine the thawed berries, sugar (if using sugar substitute, add it after heating), and cornstarch. Cook and stir over medium heat until thickened and bubbly; cook and stir for 1 minute more. Transfer to a small bowl. (If using sugar substitute, stir it in now.) Cool. Cover and chill until ready to use.

4 To serve, remove side of the springform pan. Cut the ice cream-topped brownie into 12 wedges. Top each wedge with raspberry sauce. If desired, drizzle with chocolate syrup and garnish with fresh raspberries.

*SUGAR SUBSTITUTES: Choose from Splenda Granular or Sweet'N Low bulk or packets. Follow package directions to use product amount equivalent to 3 tablespoons sugar.

PER SERVING: 198 cal., 10 g total fat (1 g sat. fat), 3 mg chol., 118 mg sodium, 33 g carb. (4 g fiber, 5 g sugars), 3 g pro. Exchanges: 1 starch, 1 carb., 1.5 fat.

PER SERVING WITH SUBSTITUTE: Same as above, except 187 cal., 30 g carb. (2 g sugars).

Cranberry Champagne Coconut Snowballs

To quickly chop the cranberries, pull out your food processor and use a couple on-off turns to evenly chop.

SERVINGS 25 (1 cake ball each)
CARB. PER SERVING 23 g
PREP 50 minutes
FREEZE 1 hour
CHILL 1 hour

1 16-ounce package angel food cake mix

Sweet sparkling wine*

1 8-ounce package reduced-fat cream cheese (Neufchâtel), softened

2 6-ounce cartons vanilla fat-free, sugar-free yogurt

1 cup fresh cranberries, very finely chopped

1½ cups frozen light whipped dessert topping, thawed

2 cups flaked or shredded coconut

Sugared whole cranberries** (optional)

Fresh mint leaves (optional)

> **PER SERVING:** 156 cal., 5 g total fat (4 g sat. fat), 7 mg chol., 210 mg sodium, 23 g carb. (1 g fiber, 16 g sugars), 3 g pro. Exchanges: 1 starch, 0.5 carb., 1 fat.

1 | Prepare the cake mix according to package directions, except substitute sparkling wine for the liquid in the cake. Use any suggested pan size and bake according to package directions. Cool cake on a wire rack. Line trays or baking pans with waxed paper; set aside.

2 | In a very large mixing bowl beat cream cheese with an electric mixer on medium speed until smooth. Beat in 1 carton of the yogurt until smooth. Stir in chopped cranberries. Crumble cake into the cream cheese mixture. Beat until combined. Drop cake mixture into 25 mounds on prepared trays or pans, using about 3 tablespoons (#20 scoop) cake mixture for each mound. Roll mounds into balls. Freeze for 1 hour or until cake balls are firm.

3 | Line a baking sheet with waxed paper; set aside. In a medium bowl fold together the remaining carton of yogurt and the dessert topping. Working with one cake ball at a time, insert a fork gently into each ball. Spread a very thin layer of the yogurt mixture over each ball, leaving the base of each ball unfrosted. Sprinkle coconut evenly over the frosted balls. Using a flat metal spatula, gently slide the cake ball off and place on prepared baking sheet. Repeat with remaining cake balls, yogurt mixture, and coconut. Chill for 1 to 24 hours.

4 | To serve, place snowballs on a cake plate and, if desired, garnish with sugared whole cranberries and fresh mint leaves.

*TEST KITCHEN TIP: For a nonalcoholic version of this recipe, prepare the angel food cake with water as the package directs.

**SUGARED WHOLE CRANBERRIES: Place cranberries in the freezer for 1 hour. Remove and immediately roll in granulated sugar.

MAKE-AHEAD DIRECTIONS: If desired, prepare as directed through Step 3. Store in a covered container. Freeze for up to 1 month. Let stand at room temperature for 30 minutes before serving. Serve as directed.

Snickerdoodle Custard Pie

A sugar and spice mixture gets sprinkled over the cooled pie, coating it like the favorite old-fashioned cookie.

SERVINGS 12 (1 wedge each)
CARB. PER SERVING 21 g
PREP 30 minutes
COOL 2 hours
BAKE 1 hour 9 minutes

½ of a 15-ounce package rolled refrigerated unbaked piecrust (1 crust)

1 ounce bittersweet chocolate, melted

1 cup refrigerated or frozen egg product, thawed, or 4 eggs

⅓ cup sugar*

2 teaspoons vanilla

¼ teaspoon ground cinnamon

⅛ teaspoon salt

⅛ teaspoon ground nutmeg

2 cups fat-free half-and-half

1 teaspoon sugar*

½ teaspoon unsweetened cocoa powder

⅛ teaspoon ground cinnamon

⅛ teaspoon ground nutmeg

1 ounce bittersweet chocolate, melted

1 Preheat oven to 450°F. Let piecrust stand according to package directions. Unroll piecrust; place into a 9-inch pie plate. Fold under extra piecrust even with the plate's edge and flute edge. Evenly prick bottom and sides of piecrust with a fork. Line piecrust with a double thickness of foil.

2 Bake for 8 minutes. Remove foil. Bake for 4 to 6 minutes more or until crust is lightly browned. Remove from oven. Cool on a wire rack. Reduce oven temperature to 350°F. Once piecrust is cooled, spread or brush 1 ounce of melted chocolate evenly over the bottom and sides of the piecrust. Let stand until chocolate is set.

3 For filling, in a medium bowl lightly beat egg with a fork. Stir in ⅓ cup sugar, the vanilla, ¼ teaspoon cinnamon, the salt, and ⅛ teaspoon nutmeg. Gradually whisk in half-and-half until mixture is well combined. Place the baked piecrust on the oven rack. Carefully pour filling into the piecrust (pie will be full). To prevent overbrowning, cover edge of pie with foil.

4 Bake for 55 to 60 minutes or until a 1-inch area around outside edge is puffed and set (center will still be jiggly and appear undone). Remove foil. Cool completely on a wire rack (pie will set upon cooling); cover and chill within 2 hours.

5 In a small bowl combine 1 teaspoon sugar, ½ teaspoon cocoa powder, ⅛ teaspoon cinnamon, and ⅛ teaspoon nutmeg. Sprinkle the spice mixture over the cooled or chilled pie. To serve, cut into 12 wedges. Drizzle each serving with some of the remaining 1 ounce melted bittersweet chocolate.**

*SUGAR SUBSTITUTES: We do not recommend using a sugar substitute for this recipe.

**TEST KITCHEN TIP: To drizzle chocolate, place melted chocolate in a resealable plastic bag; seal bag. Snip off corner of bag and squeeze to drizzle chocolate over individual wedges.

PER SERVING: 149 cal., 6 g total fat (3 g sat. fat), 4 mg chol., 191 mg sodium, 21 g carb. (0 g fiber, 10 g sugars), 4 g pro. Exchanges: 0.5 starch, 1 carb., 1 fat.

Our Best Traditional Pumpkin Pie

This health-smart Thanksgiving favorite promises everything the classic pie presents, minus the extra calories and fat.

SERVINGS 10 (1 wedge each)
CARB. PER SERVING 30 g or 24 g
PREP 30 minutes
BAKE 40 minutes

1 recipe Oil Pastry

1 15-ounce can pumpkin

1/3 cup sugar*

2 tablespoons honey

1 teaspoon ground cinnamon

1/4 teaspoon ground ginger

1/4 teaspoon ground nutmeg

1/2 cup refrigerated or frozen egg product, thawed, or 2 eggs, lightly beaten

1 teaspoon vanilla

3/4 cup evaporated fat-free milk

Frozen light whipped dessert topping, thawed (optional)

Ground cinnamon or ground nutmeg (optional)

PER SERVING: 187 cal., 6 g total fat (1 g sat. fat), 0 mg chol., 111 mg sodium, 30 g carb. (2 g fiber, 15 g sugars), 5 g pro. Exchanges: 1.5 starch, 0.5 carb., 1 fat.

PER SERVING WITH SUBSTITUTE: Same as above, except 164 cal., 24 g carb. (9 g sugars). Exchanges: 0 carb.

1 Preheat oven to 375°F. Prepare Oil Pastry. On a well-floured surface slightly flatten the pastry dough. Roll dough into a circle about 12 inches in diameter. Transfer pastry onto a 9-inch pie plate. Ease pastry into pie plate, being careful not to stretch pastry. Trim pastry to 1/2 inch beyond edge of pie plate. Fold under extra pastry. Flute or crimp edge as desired. Do not prick pastry.

2 Combine pumpkin, sugar, honey, the 1 teaspoon cinnamon, the ginger, and the 1/4 teaspoon nutmeg. Add egg and vanilla. Beat with a fork just until combined. Stir in evaporated milk. Pour pumpkin mixture into pastry shell.

3 Cover edge of the pie with foil. Bake for 20 minutes. Remove foil. Bake for 20 to 25 minutes more or until filling appears set (edges of filling may crack slightly).

4 Cool on a wire rack. Cover and chill within 2 hours. To serve, cut into 10 wedges. If desired, serve with dessert topping and sprinkle with additional cinnamon and/or nutmeg.

OIL PASTRY: In a bowl combine 1 1/3 cups all-purpose flour and 1/4 teaspoon salt. Add 1/4 cup vegetable oil and 1/4 cup fat-free milk to flour mixture. Stir with a fork until combined (dough will appear crumbly). Use your hands to gently work dough into a ball.

*SUGAR SUBSTITUTES: Choose from Splenda Granular or Sweet'N Low bulk or packets. Follow package directions to use product amount equivalent to 1/3 cup sugar.

Hazelnut-Crusted Mascarpone Cheesecake

Mascarpone cheese is a soft Italian dessert cheese usually sold in a tublike container. Look for it in the cheese section of the supermarket.

SERVINGS 16 (1 wedge each)
CARB. PER SERVING 17 g or 12 g
PREP 35 minutes
BAKE 1 hour
COOL 45 minutes
CHILL 4 hours

- 1 cup finely crushed low-fat graham crackers (13 to 14 squares)
- ¼ cup coarsely ground toasted hazelnuts*
- ¼ teaspoon ground allspice
- ⅓ cup light butter, melted
- 2 8-ounce packages fat-free cream cheese, softened
- 1 8-ounce package mascarpone cheese, softened
- ⅔ cup sugar**
- 3 tablespoons fat-free milk
- 1½ teaspoons vanilla
- 3 egg whites, lightly beaten
- 1 ounce bittersweet or dark chocolate, melted (optional)
- 3 tablespoons pomegranate seeds (optional)

1 | Preheat oven to 325°F. For crust, in a medium bowl stir together crushed graham crackers, hazelnuts, and allspice. Stir in butter. Press crumb mixture onto bottom and about 1 inch up the sides of an 8-inch springform pan; set aside.

2 | In a large mixing bowl beat cream cheese until smooth. Beat in mascarpone cheese, sugar, milk, and vanilla with an electric mixer on medium speed until well combined. Add egg whites. Beat on low speed just until combined (do not overbeat).

3 | Pour filling into crust-lined pan. Place on a shallow baking pan. Bake for 60 to 70 minutes or until center appears nearly set when shaken gently.

4 | Cool in the pan on a wire rack for 15 minutes. Use a sharp, thin-bladed knife to loosen the crust from the sides of the pan; cool for 30 minutes more. Remove the sides of the pan; cool cheesecake completely. Cover and chill at least 4 hours before serving.

5 | If desired, drizzle top of cooled cheesecake with melted chocolate and garnish with pomegranate seeds.

*TEST KITCHEN TIP: To toast hazelnuts, spread the nuts in a shallow baking pan. Bake in a 350°F oven for 8 to 10 minutes or until toasted, watching carefully to avoid burning and stirring once or twice. Cool slightly. Transfer hazelnuts to a clean kitchen towel. Rub hazelnuts vigorously with the towel to remove the papery skins.

**SUGAR SUBSTITUTE: Choose Splenda Sugar Blend for Baking. Follow package directions to use product amount equivalent to ⅔ cup sugar. Decrease baking time of cheesecake to 50 to 60 minutes.

PER SERVING: 178 cal., 10 g total fat (5 g sat. fat), 27 mg chol., 278 mg sodium, 17 g carb. (1 g fiber, 11 g sugars), 6 g pro. Exchanges: 0.5 starch, 0.5 carb., 0.5 lean meat, 2 fat.

PER SERVING WITH SUBSTITUTE: Same as above, except 166 cal., 12 g carb. (7 g sugars).

Almond-Tangerine Panna Cotta

Use a butter knife to carefully loosen the jiggly gelatin dessert from the cup, then invert it onto the dessert plate to release.

SERVINGS 4 (1 custard cup each)
CARB. PER SERVING 29 g or 18 g
PREP 25 minutes
CHILL 4 hours

3	tablespoons sugar*
1½	teaspoons unflavored gelatin
1	cup fat-free milk
1	cup plain Greek yogurt
½	teaspoon almond extract
1	tablespoon sugar*
1	teaspoon cornstarch
⅓	cup pomegranate or cranberry juice
½	cup tangerine sections (3 to 4 tangerines)
2	tablespoons snipped dried tart cherries

PER SERVING: 157 cal., 2 g total fat (1 g sat. fat), 5 mg chol., 52 mg sodium, 29 g carb. (1 g fiber, 26 g sugars), 9 g pro. Exchanges: 1 fruit, 1 carb., 1 lean meat, 0.5 fat.

PER SERVING WITH SUBSTITUTE: Same as above, except 114 cal., 18 g carb. (15 g sugars). Exchanges: 0 carb.

1 | Place four 6-ounce custard cups or ramekins in a shallow baking pan; set aside. In a small saucepan stir together 3 tablespoons sugar and the gelatin. Stir in milk. Heat over medium heat until gelatin is dissolved, stirring frequently. Remove from heat. Whisk in yogurt and ¼ teaspoon of the almond extract until smooth. Pour mixture into custard cups. Cover and chill for 4 to 24 hours or until set.

2 | For sauce, in a small saucepan stir together 1 tablespoon sugar and the cornstarch. Stir in pomegranate juice. Cook and stir over medium heat until thickened and bubbly. Remove from heat. Stir in tangerine sections, cherries, and the remaining ¼ teaspoon almond extract. Cool.

3 | To serve, immerse bottom halves of custard cups in hot water for 10 seconds. Using a small sharp knife, loosen panna cotta from sides of cups. Invert a serving plate over each cup; turn plate and cup over together. Remove cups. Serve panna cotta with sauce.

*****SUGAR SUBSTITUTE:** Choose Splenda Granular. Follow package directions to use product amounts equivalent to 3 tablespoons and 1 tablespoon sugar.

Oatmeal-Banana Bread Pudding

Jump-start your morning cooking the day before. Dry the bread cubes and store them in an airtight container overnight.

SERVINGS 9 ($^1/_2$ cup each)
CARB. PER SERVING 24 g or 20 g
PREP 25 minutes
BAKE 45 minutes

4 egg whites, lightly beaten

2 cups fat-free milk

3 tablespoons packed brown sugar*

1 teaspoon vanilla

$^1/_2$ teaspoon pumpkin pie spice

5 cups dried light-style oatmeal bread cubes**

1 large banana, halved lengthwise and sliced

$^1/_4$ cup chopped walnuts or pecans, toasted

$^1/_4$ cup miniature semisweet chocolate pieces

1 Preheat oven to 350°F. In a large bowl combine egg whites, milk, brown sugar, vanilla, and pumpkin pie spice. Add bread cubes, banana, nuts, and chocolate pieces; toss gently to combine. Transfer to an ungreased 1$^1/_2$-quart casserole.

2 Bake, uncovered, for 45 to 50 minutes or until a knife inserted near the center comes out clean. Spoon the pudding into nine dessert dishes and serve while warm.

*SUGAR SUBSTITUTES: Choose from Sweet'N Low Brown or Sugar Twin Granulated Brown. Follow package directions to use product amount equivalent to 3 tablespoons brown sugar.

**TEST KITCHEN TIP: Start with 8 slices (5.5 ounces) of light-style oatmeal bread. To dry bread cubes, preheat oven to 300°F. Spread bread cubes in a single layer in a shallow baking pan. Bake for 10 to 15 minutes or until dried, stirring twice. Cool completely.

PER SERVING: 155 cal., 4 g total fat (1 g sat. fat), 1 mg chol., 126 mg sodium, 24 g carb. (1 g fiber, 14 g sugars), 6 g pro. Exchanges: 1 starch, 0.5 carb.,

PER SERVING WITH SUBSTITUTE: Same as above, except 137 cal., 125 mg sodium, 20 g carb. (9 g sugars). Exchanges: 0 carb., 0.5 lean meat, 0.5 fat.

Berries with Custard Sauce

Use a bowl large enough to hold half of the hot milk mixture when combining it with the egg.

SERVINGS 4 ($^1/_2$ cup berries and $^1/_4$ cup custard sauce each)
CARB. PER SERVING 19 g
PREP 20 minutes
CHILL 2 hours

2 tablespoons sugar*

2 teaspoons cornstarch

$^3/_4$ cup fat-free milk

1 egg, beaten

$^1/_4$ cup light sour cream

2 tablespoons sweet or dry Marsala

2 cups fresh berries, such as raspberries, blackberries, blueberries, or halved strawberries, and/or quartered fresh figs

Fresh mint leaves (optional)

1 | For custard, in a heavy small saucepan combine sugar and cornstarch. Stir in milk. Cook and stir over medium heat until thickened and bubbly. Cook and stir for 2 minutes more. Remove from heat. Gradually stir about half of the hot milk mixture into the beaten egg. Return all of the egg mixture to the saucepan. Cook and stir until nearly bubbly, but do not boil. Immediately pour custard into a bowl; stir in sour cream and Marsala. Cover surface with plastic wrap. Chill the custard for at least 2 hours or up to 24 hours.

2 | To serve, divide the berries and/or figs evenly among four dessert dishes. Spoon custard over fruit. If desired, garnish with mint leaves. Serve immediately.

*SUGAR SUBSTITUTES: We do not recommend using a sugar substitute for this recipe.

PER SERVING: 125 cal., 3 g total fat (1 g sat. fat), 52 mg chol., 46 mg sodium, 19 g carb. (4 g fiber, 12 g sugars), 4 g pro. Exchanges: 1 fruit, 0.5 carb., 1 fat.

3 grams fat

QUICK TIP

Although they won't be as plump and perfect as fresh-picked, you can substitute frozen mixed berries for the fresh berries. Thaw the berries and drain well before dividing them among the dessert dishes.

Banana Pudding with Shaved Dark Chocolate

A blender makes preparing this silky-smooth no-cook pudding a breeze. Add the ingredients to the blender and blend, scraping down the sides as necessary.

SERVINGS 4 ($^1/_2$ cup each)
CARB. PER SERVING 29 g
PREP 10 minutes
CHILL 1 hour

2 ripe bananas

1 cup silken-style tofu (fresh bean curd) (8 ounces)

2 tablespoons light agave nectar

1 teaspoon vanilla

Dash ground cinnamon

1$^1/_2$ ounces shaved dark chocolate

5 grams protein

PER SERVING: 179 cal., 5 g total fat (2 g sat. fat), 1 mg chol., 24 mg sodium, 29 g carb. (2 g fiber, 21 g sugars), 5 g pro. Exchanges: 1 fruit, 1 carb., 0.5 lean meat, 1 fat.

1 In a blender combine banana, tofu, agave nectar, vanilla, and cinnamon. Cover and blend until smooth. Pour or spoon into four individual serving bowls. Top with shaved dark chocolate. Cover loosely and chill for at least 1 hour or up to 4 hours before serving.

Pear Crunch with Lemon Cream and Blue Cheese

Uncooked quinoa adds extra crunch to a classic streusel topping of walnuts, rolled oats, sugar, cinnamon, and butter.

SERVINGS 10 ($^1/_2$ cup fruit mixture and a scant 2 tablespoons lemon cream each)
CARB. PER SERVING 30 g or 27 g
PREP 35 minutes
BAKE 35 minutes
COOL 30 minutes

- 6 medium firm ripe Bartlett or D'Anjou pears, peeled if desired, quartered, cored, and thinly sliced
- 2 tablespoons flour
- $^1/_4$ teaspoon ground cardamom
- $^1/_8$ teaspoon ground nutmeg
- $1^1/_2$ tablespoons honey
- $^1/_2$ cup chopped walnuts
- $^1/_3$ cup rolled oats
- 3 tablespoons uncooked quinoa, rinsed and well drained
- 2 tablespoons packed brown sugar*
- $^1/_4$ teaspoon ground cinnamon
- $^1/_8$ teaspoon salt
- 3 tablespoons light butter
- $^1/_3$ cup light tub-style cream cheese, softened
- 1 tablespoon fat-free milk
- 1 teaspoon finely shredded lemon peel
- $^1/_8$ teaspoon ground cardamom
- $^3/_4$ cup frozen light whipped dessert topping, thawed
- $^1/_2$ cup crumbled reduced-fat blue cheese (optional)

PER SERVING: 197 cal., 8 g total fat (3 g sat. fat), 9 mg chol., 102 mg sodium, 30 g carb. (4 g fiber, 17 g sugars), 3 g pro. Exchanges: 1 fruit, 0.5 starch, 0.5 carb., 1.5 fat.

PER SERVING WITH SUBSTITUTE: Same as above, except 186 cal., 27 g carb. (14 g sugars), 101 mg sodium.

1 Preheat oven to 375°F. In a large bowl combine pear slices, flour, $^1/_4$ teaspoon cardamom, and the nutmeg. Toss to coat. Drizzle with honey and toss to combine. Spread fruit mixture into an even layer in a 2-quart square, oval, or rectangular baking dish.

2 In a medium bowl combine walnuts, oats, quinoa, brown sugar, cinnamon, and salt. Using a pastry blender, cut in light butter until mixture resembles coarse crumbs. Crumble evenly over pear mixture in dish.

3 Cover and bake for 10 minutes. Uncover and bake for 25 to 35 minutes more or until pears are tender and topping is browned. Cool on a wire rack about 30 minutes

4 For lemon cream, in a medium bowl beat cream cheese and milk with an electric mixer on low speed until smooth. Stir in lemon peel and $^1/_8$ teaspoon cardamom. Fold in dessert topping.

5 To serve, spoon pear crunch into 10 dessert dishes. Top each serving with a spoonful of lemon cream. If desired, sprinkle with blue cheese.

*SUGAR SUBSTITUTES: Choose from Sweet'N Low Brown or Sugar Twin Brown. Follow package directions to use product amount equivalent to 2 tablespoons brown sugar.

Salted Caramel Pistachio-Apricot Baklava

Make sure to use butter-flavor nonstick cooking spray to increase the butter flavor while decreasing the amount of butter used to create flaky layers.

SERVINGS 24 (1 piece each)
CARB. PER SERVING 18 g
PREP 45 minutes
BAKE 45 minutes

1½ cups boiling water

1 cup finely chopped dried apricots

1½ cups shelled lightly salted pistachio
     nuts, finely chopped

2 tablespoons packed brown sugar*

2 teaspoons finely shredded
     lemon peel

Butter-flavor nonstick cooking spray

3 tablespoons butter, melted

½ of a 16-ounce package frozen
     phyllo dough (14×9-inch
     rectangles), thawed

⅔ cup packed brown sugar*

⅛ teaspoon ground nutmeg

1 teaspoon kosher salt

PER SERVING: 127 cal., 6 g total fat (1 g sat. fat),
4 mg chol., 176 mg sodium, 18 g carb. (1 g fiber,
11 g sugars), 3 g pro. Exchanges: 1 starch, 1 fat.

1 Preheat oven to 325°F. In a medium bowl combine boiling water and apricots. Let stand for 5 minutes. Strain apricots through a fine-mesh sieve, reserving the liquid and gently pressing on apricots with the back of a large spoon to remove as much liquid as possible. In a large bowl stir together drained apricots, the pistachios, 2 tablespoons brown sugar, and the lemon peel. Set aside.

2 Coat the bottom of a 13×9×2-inch baking pan with cooking spray. Unroll phyllo dough (keep phyllo covered with plastic wrap until needed). Layer 5 or 6 phyllo sheets in the prepared baking pan, lightly coating the tops of the sheets with cooking spray except for every third sheet, which should be brushed with melted butter. Sprinkle with about one-third of the nut mixture. Repeat layering phyllo sheets and sprinkling with nut mixture two more times, coating the top of each phyllo sheet with cooking spray or melted butter.

3 Layer the remaining phyllo sheets on top of filling, coating each sheet with cooking spray or butter. Brush the final sheet with butter. Using a sharp knife, cut stacked layers into 24 diamond- or rectangular-shape pieces.

4 Bake about 45 minutes or until golden brown. Cool slightly in pan on a wire rack.

5 Meanwhile, measure the drained apricot soaking liquid. Discard enough of the liquid or add water to the liquid to make ⅔ cup total liquid. In a small saucepan stir together the ⅔ cup apricot soaking liquid, ⅔ cup brown sugar, and the nutmeg. Bring to boiling; reduce heat. Simmer, uncovered, for 10 minutes or until reduced to about ⅓ cup. Pour the syrup evenly over slightly cooled baklava in the pan. Sprinkle top evenly with coarse salt. Recut diamonds or rectangles to serve.

*SUGAR SUBSTITUTES: We do not recommend using a sugar substitute for this recipe.

Red Velvet Pumpkin Bars

If you have a small cookie scoop in the drawer, pull it out to use for topping each cakelike square.

SERVINGS 24 (1 bar and 1 tablespoon topping each)
CARB. PER SERVING 24 g or 18 g
PREP 30 minutes
BAKE 25 minutes

Nonstick cooking spray

2 teaspoons all-purpose flour

1½ cups all-purpose flour

1⅓ cups granulated sugar*

½ cup whole wheat flour

3 tablespoons unsweetened cocoa powder

1 teaspoon baking soda

½ teaspoon salt

½ teaspoon pumpkin pie spice

1 15-ounce can pumpkin

1 5- to 6-ounce carton plain fat-free Greek yogurt

½ cup refrigerated or frozen egg product, thawed

⅓ cup canola oil

1 tablespoon red food coloring

1½ teaspoons vanilla

1 teaspoon cider vinegar

1 1-ounce envelope whipped dessert topping mix

¼ cup whipped light cream cheese

3 tablespoons fat-free milk

2 tablespoons powdered sugar

½ teaspoon vanilla

Unsweetened cocoa powder (optional)

1 Preheat oven to 350°F. Coat a 15×10×1-inch baking pan with cooking spray. Gently wipe the pan interior with a paper towel so the pan bottom and sides are evenly coated with the spray. Dust with the 2 teaspoons all-purpose flour; set aside.

2 In a large bowl sift together the 1½ cups all-purpose flour, the granulated sugar, whole wheat flour, the 3 tablespoons cocoa powder, the baking soda, salt, and pumpkin pie spice.

3 In a medium bowl combine pumpkin, yogurt, egg, oil, food coloring, the 1½ teaspoons vanilla, and the vinegar. Add to flour mixture, stirring just until combined. Spread in the prepared baking pan.

4 Bake for 25 to 30 minutes or until a toothpick inserted near the center comes out clean. Cool in pan on a wire rack. Cut into 24 bars.

5 For topping, in a medium bowl combine topping mix, cream cheese, milk, powdered sugar, and the ½ teaspoon vanilla. Beat with an electric mixer on high speed until stiff peaks form (tips stand straight). Cover and chill until needed.

6 To serve, cut into 24 bars. Top each bar with a tablespoon-size spoonful of the topping. If desired, sprinkle with additional cocoa powder.

*SUGAR SUBSTITUTES: Choose from Splenda Sugar Blend for Baking or C&H Light Sugar & Stevia Blend. Follow package directions to use product amount equivalent to 1⅓ cups granulated sugar.

PER SERVING: 137 cal., 4 g total fat (1 g sat. fat), 1 mg chol., 128 mg sodium, 24 g carb. (1 g fiber, 14 g sugars), 3 g pro. Exchanges: 1.5 starch, 1 fat.

PER SERVING WITH SUBSTITUTE: Same as above, except 120 cal., 18 g carb. (8 g sugars). Exchanges: 1 starch.

Maple-Bourbon Chocolate Tiramisu with Pecans

This creamy, dreamy, and delicious version of the Italian specialty is the ultimate dessert. You can use hazelnuts or walnuts in place of pecans.

SERVINGS 12 (1 portion each)
CARB. PER SERVING 18 g
PREP 35 minutes
CHILL 4 hours

⅓ cup boiling water

2 tablespoons instant espresso coffee powder

⅓ cup light maple-flavored syrup

2 tablespoons bourbon (optional)

6 ounces reduced-fat cream cheese (Neufchâtel), softened

3 tablespoons fat-free milk

1 teaspoon vanilla

⅔ cup frozen light whipped dessert topping, thawed

2 3-ounce packages ladyfingers, split

1½ cups prepared fat-free, sugar-free chocolate pudding*

⅓ cup chopped pecans, toasted

Dark chocolate curls (optional)

1 | For syrup mixture, in a small bowl combine boiling water and espresso powder; stir to dissolve espresso powder. Stir in maple syrup and bourbon (if using). Set aside.

2 | In a medium bowl beat cream cheese with an electric mixer on low speed until smooth. Add milk and vanilla and beat until smooth. Fold in dessert topping. Set aside.

3 | Arrange half of the ladyfinger halves in the bottom of a 2-quart rectangular baking dish. Brush with half of the syrup mixture. Top with chocolate pudding, spreading to an even layer. Top with remaining ladyfingers. Brush with remaining syrup mixture. Top with cream cheese mixture, spreading to an even layer. Cover and chill for 4 to 24 hours.

4 | To serve, cut into 12 portions. Sprinkle each serving with pecans. If desired, garnish with chocolate curls.

*TEST KITCHEN TIP: For easy pudding, use a 4-serving-size package fat-free, sugar-free, reduced-calorie chocolate instant pudding mix. Prepare according to package directions; measure 1½ cups to use in the tiramisu.

18 grams carb

PER SERVING: 154 cal., 7 g total fat (3 g sat. fat), 42 mg chol., 180 mg sodium, 18 g carb. (1 g fiber, 9 g sugars), 5 g pro. Exchanges: 1 starch, 0.5 lean meat, 1 fat.

Stuffed Pumpkin Cookie Crescents

These little half-moon pockets are stuffed with a spiced pumpkin filling. Divide the extra pumpkin into $^1/_2$-cup portions and freeze for other uses.

SERVINGS 24 (1 cookie each)
CARB. PER SERVING 14 g
PREP 30 minutes
CHILL 1 hour
BAKE 12 minutes per batch

$^1/_4$ cup butter, softened

$^1/_4$ cup olive oil

$^1/_2$ cup powdered sugar*

$^1/_4$ cup plain fat-free Greek yogurt

$^1/_4$ cup refrigerated or frozen egg product, thawed

$^1/_4$ teaspoon almond extract

2 cups flour

$^1/_4$ teaspoon baking soda

$^1/_4$ teaspoon salt

$^1/_2$ cup canned pumpkin

$^1/_4$ cup packed brown sugar*

1 teaspoon pumpkin pie spice

$^1/_8$ teaspoon salt

1 egg white, lightly beaten

2 tablespoons coarse sugar or granulated sugar*

$^1/_2$ teaspoon ground cinnamon

1 In a large bowl combine the butter and olive oil. Beat with an electric mixer on medium speed until combined. Add the powdered sugar, yogurt, egg, and almond extract, beating until well mixed and scraping sides of bowl occasionally.

2 In a medium bowl stir together flour, baking soda, and salt. Add to beaten mixture; beat until well mixed. Divide dough in half, forming each half into a disk. Wrap each disk in plastic wrap. Chill in the refrigerator about 1 hour or until dough is easy to handle.

3 Meanwhile, for pumpkin filling, in a medium bowl stir together pumpkin, brown sugar, pumpkin pie spice, and salt.

4 Preheat oven to 350°F. Line cookie sheets with parchment paper. On a lightly floured surface roll dough disks, one at a time, to $^1/_8$-inch thickness. Using a 3-inch fluted round cookie cutter, cut into rounds. Place on prepared cookie sheets.

5 Place 1 teaspoon of the pumpkin filling on half of each dough round. Fold dough over to cover filling. Press edges with the tines of a fork to seal. Brush tops with egg white; sprinkle with the coarse sugar and cinnamon. Bake for 12 to 14 minutes or until bottoms are lightly browned. Transfer to a wire rack and let cool.

*SUGAR SUBSTITUTES: We do not recommend using a sugar substitute for any of the sugars in this recipe.

PER SERVING: 103 cal., 4 g total fat (2 g sat. fat), 5 mg chol., 76 mg sodium, 14 g carb. (0 g fiber, 6 g sugars), 2 g pro. Exchanges: 1 starch, 1 fat.

Molasses Cookies

The rich molasses flavor comes from the dark brown sugar and molasses combo, so don't substitute light brown sugar.

SERVINGS 48 (1 cookie each)
CARB. PER SERVING 9 g or 7 g
PREP 30 minutes
CHILL 1 hour
BAKE 7 minutes per batch

$\frac{1}{3}$ cup margarine, softened

$\frac{2}{3}$ cup packed dark brown sugar*

1 teaspoon baking soda

1 teaspoon ground ginger

$\frac{1}{2}$ teaspoon ground cinnamon

$\frac{1}{4}$ cup refrigerated or frozen egg product, thawed, or 1 egg

$\frac{1}{4}$ cup mild molasses

$1\frac{1}{2}$ cups all-purpose flour

$\frac{1}{2}$ cup white whole wheat flour

Nonstick cooking spray

2 tablespoons granulated sugar*

$\frac{1}{2}$ teaspoon ground cinnamon

PER SERVING: 48 cal., 1 g total fat (0 g sat. fat), 0 mg chol., 45 mg sodium, 9 g carb. (0 g fiber, 5 g sugars), 1 g pro. Exchanges: 0.5 starch.

PER SERVING WITH SUBSTITUTE: Same as above, except 44 cal., 7 g carb. (3 g sugars), 44 mg sodium.

1 | In a large mixing bowl beat margarine with an electric mixer on medium to high speed for 30 seconds. Add brown sugar, baking soda, ginger, and $\frac{1}{2}$ teaspoon cinnamon. Beat mixture until combined. Beat in egg and molasses. Beat in as much of the all-purpose flour and white whole wheat flour as you can with the mixer. Stir in any remaining flour with a wooden spoon. Cover and refrigerate for 1 hour.

2 | Lightly coat cookie sheet with cooking spray; set aside. Preheat oven to 350°F.

3 | Shape dough into balls that are slightly less than 1 inch in diameter. In a small dish combine the granulated sugar and $\frac{1}{2}$ teaspoon cinnamon. Roll balls in sugar-cinnamon mixture. Place balls 2 inches apart on prepared cookie sheet. Flatten each ball to a $\frac{1}{2}$-inch thickness with bottom of a glass, dipping glass in the sugar mixture if it sticks. Bake about 7 minutes or until edges are set. Remove from cookie sheet; transfer cookies to a wire rack and let cool.

*SUGAR SUBSTITUTE: Choose Splenda Brown Sugar Baking Blend for the brown sugar. Follow package directions to use product amount equivalent to $\frac{2}{3}$ cup brown sugar. Baking time may need to be decreased slightly. We do not recommend using a substitute for granulated sugar used to coat the cookies.

Soft Sugar Cookies

Place these cookies in a freezer container and stash them in the freezer to pull out when unexpected guests stop by.

SERVINGS 48 (1 cookie each)
CARB. PER SERVING 11 g or 7 g
PREP 25 minutes
BAKE 14 minutes per batch
COOL 1 minute

½ cup butter, softened

4 ounces cream cheese, softened

1¾ cups sugar*

1 teaspoon baking soda

1 teaspoon cream of tartar

⅛ teaspoon salt

3 egg yolks

½ teaspoon vanilla

1¼ cups all-purpose flour

½ cup white whole wheat flour

PER SERVING: 73 cal., 3 g total fat (2 g sat. fat), 19 mg chol., 57 mg sodium, 11 g carb. (0 g fiber, 7 g sugars), 1 g pro. Exchanges: 0.5 starch, 0.5 fat.

PER SERVING WITH SUBSTITUTE: Same as above, except 62 cal., 7 g carb. (4 g sugars).

1 Preheat oven to 300°F. In a large mixing bowl beat butter and cream cheese with an electric mixer on medium to high speed for 30 seconds. Add sugar, baking soda, cream of tartar, and salt. Beat mixture until combined, scraping sides of bowl occasionally. Beat in egg yolks and vanilla. Beat in as much of the all-purpose flour and white whole wheat flour as you can with the mixer. Stir in any remaining flour with a wooden spoon.

2 Shape dough into balls that are 1 inch in diameter. Place balls 2 inches apart on ungreased cookie sheets.

3 Bake for 14 to 16 minutes or until edges are set; do not let edges brown. Cool cookies for 1 minute on cookie sheet. Transfer cookies to a wire rack and let cool.

*SUGAR SUBSTITUTES: Choose from Splenda Sugar Blend for Baking or Sun Crystals Granulated Blend. Follow package directions to use product amount equivalent to 1¾ cups sugar. Bake as directed, except reduce baking time to 12 to 14 minutes.

recipe index

recipe guide

See how we calculate nutrition information to help you count calories, carbs, and serving sizes.

Inside Our Recipes

Precise serving sizes (listed below the recipe title) help you to manage portions.

Ingredients listed as optional are not included in the per-serving nutrition analysis.

When kitchen basics such as ice, salt, black pepper, and nonstick cooking spray are not listed in the ingredients list, they are italicized in the directions.

Ingredients
• Tub-style vegetable oil spread refers to 60% to 70% vegetable oil product.
• Lean ground beef refers to 95% or leaner ground beef.

Nutrition Information

Nutrition facts per serving and food exchanges are noted with each recipe.

Test Kitchen tips and sugar substitutes are listed after the recipe directions.

When ingredient choices appear, we use the first one to calculate the nutrition analysis.

Key to Abbreviations

cal. = calories
sat. fat = saturated fat
chol. = cholesterol
carb. = carbohydrate
pro. = protein

metric information

The charts on this page provide a guide for converting measurements from the U.S. customary system, which is used throughout this book, to the metric system.

Product Differences

Most of the ingredients called for in the recipes in this book are available in most countries. However, some are known by different names. Here are some common American ingredients and their possible counterparts:

* All-purpose flour is enriched, bleached or unbleached white household flour. When self-rising flour is used in place of all-purpose flour in a recipe that calls for leavening, omit the leavening agent (baking soda or baking powder) and salt.
* Baking soda is bicarbonate of soda.
* Cornstarch is cornflour.
* Golden raisins are sultanas.
* Light-color corn syrup is golden syrup.
* Powdered sugar is icing sugar.
* Sugar (white) is granulated, fine granulated, or castor sugar.
* Vanilla or vanilla extract is vanilla essence.

Volume and Weight

The United States traditionally uses cup measures for liquid and solid ingredients. The chart below shows the approximate imperial and metric equivalents. If you are accustomed to weighing solid ingredients, the following approximate equivalents will be helpful.

* 1 cup butter, castor sugar, or rice = 8 ounces = $^1/_2$ pound = 250 grams
* 1 cup flour = 4 ounces = $^1/_4$ pound = 125 grams
* 1 cup icing sugar = 5 ounces = 150 grams

Canadian and U.S. volume for a cup measure is 8 fluid ounces (237 ml), but the standard metric equivalent is 250 ml.

1 British imperial cup is 10 fluid ounces.

In Australia, 1 tablespoon equals 20 ml, and there are 4 teaspoons in the Australian tablespoon.

Spoon measures are used for smaller amounts of ingredients. Although the size of the tablespoon varies slightly in different countries, for practical purposes and for recipes in this book, a straight substitution is all that's necessary. Measurements made using cups or spoons always should be level unless stated otherwise.

Common Weight Range Replacements

Imperial / U.S.	Metric
$^1/_2$ ounce	15 g
1 ounce	25 g or 30 g
4 ounces ($^1/_4$ pound)	115 g or 125 g
8 ounces ($^1/_2$ pound)	225 g or 250 g
16 ounces (1 pound)	450 g or 500 g
$1^1/_4$ pounds	625 g
$1^1/_2$ pounds	750 g
2 pounds or $2^1/_4$ pounds	1,000 g or 1 Kg

Oven Temperature Equivalents

Fahrenheit Setting	Celsius Setting*	Gas Setting
300°F	150°C	Gas Mark 2 (very low)
325°F	160°C	Gas Mark 3 (low)
350°F	180°C	Gas Mark 4 (moderate)
375°F	190°C	Gas Mark 5 (moderate)
400°F	200°C	Gas Mark 6 (hot)
425°F	220°C	Gas Mark 7 (hot)
450°F	230°C	Gas Mark 8 (very hot)
475°F	240°C	Gas Mark 9 (very hot)
500°F	260°C	Gas Mark 10 (extremely hot)
Broil	Broil	Grill

Electric and gas ovens may be calibrated using celsius. However, for an electric oven, increase celsius setting 10 to 20 degrees when cooking above 160°C. For convection or forced air ovens (gas or electric), lower the temperature setting 25°F/10°C when cooking at all heat levels.

Baking Pan Sizes

Imperial / U.S.	Metric
9×1$^1/_2$-inch round cake pan	22- or 23×4-cm (1.5 L)
9×1$^1/_2$-inch pie plate	22- or 23×4-cm (1 L)
8×8×2-inch square cake pan	20×5-cm (2 L)
9×9×2-inch square cake pan	22- or 23×4.5-cm (2.5 L)
11×7×1$^1/_2$-inch baking pan	28×17×4-cm (2 L)
2-quart rectangular baking pan	30×19×4.5-cm (3 L)
13×9×2-inch baking pan	34×22×4.5-cm (3.5 L)
15×10×1-inch jelly roll pan	40×25×2-cm
9×5×3-inch loaf pan	23×13×8-cm (2 L)
2-quart casserole	2 L

U.S. / Standard Metric Equivalents

$^1/_8$ teaspoon = 0.5 ml	
$^1/_4$ teaspoon = 1 ml	
$^1/_2$ teaspoon = 2 ml	
1 teaspoon = 5 ml	
1 tablespoon = 15 ml	
2 tablespoons = 25 ml	
$^1/_4$ cup = 2 fluid ounces = 50 ml	
$^1/_3$ cup = 3 fluid ounces = 75 ml	
$^1/_2$ cup = 4 fluid ounces = 125 ml	
$^2/_3$ cup = 5 fluid ounces = 150 ml	
$^3/_4$ cup = 6 fluid ounces = 175 ml	
1 cup = 8 fluid ounces = 250 ml	
2 cups = 1 pint = 500 ml	
1 quart = 1 litre	